CLONES LACE

THE STORY
AND
PATTERNS OF AN IRISH CROCHET

MÁIRE TREANOR

MERCIER PRESS

MERCIER PRESS
5 French Church Street, Cork
and
16 Hume Street, Dublin 2

Trade enquiries to COLUMBA MERCIER DISTRIBUTION,
55a Spruce Avenue, Stillorgan Industrial Park, Blackrock, Dublin

© Máire Treanor 2002

ISBN: 1 85635 383 4

10 9 8 7 6 5 4 3 2 1

WITH FOND MEMORIES OF
SADIE AND EAMON – MO MHÁTHAIR AGUS M'ATHAIR.
WHO PASSED ON THEIR IDEALISTIC LOVE OF CULTURE AND CREATIVITY TO US
GO RAIBH SIAD I MEASC NA LAOCHRA.

AGUS DO
MÁIRÉAD, ÁINE AGUS CÁIT

Illustrations by Elaine Agnew.
Photographs: Connor Tilson, Gillian Buckley, DC Photos, Nigel Savage, Suzanne Toal, Jacqui Heurst, Seán Boylan, Roy McAdoo, Aoibheann Devlin and Máire Treanor. 'Other laces' photographs courtesy of Rosemary Cathcart, Sheelin Museum, Bellinaleck, county Fermangh; Nora Finnegan, The Lace Design Centre, Kenmare, county Kerry; and Martha Hughes, Lace Gallery, Carrickmacross, county Monaghan.
Projects designed by Máire (Connolly) Treanor.

An Chomhairle Oidhreachta / The Heritage Council

THIS PUBLICATION HAS RECEIVED SUPPORT FROM THE HERITAGE COUNCIL UNDER THE 2001 PUBLICATIONS GRANT SCHEME.

OTHER SPONSORS: *Monaghan Par[...]* [...]*egion), Craft Council of Ireland, Brian Curran, Matthews of Clones, Morgan* [...]

Printed in Ireland by Colour Books Ltd.

CONTENTS

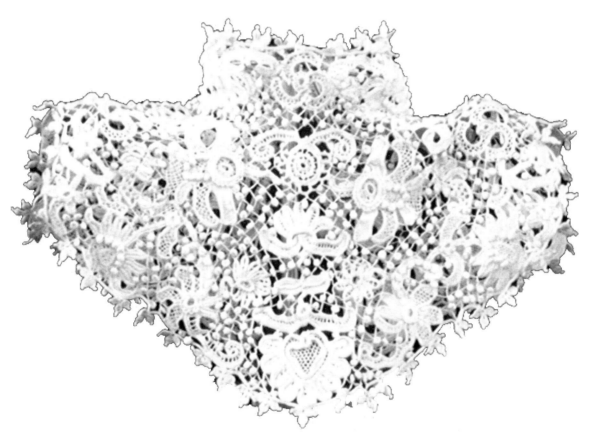

High-necked collar: courtesy of Rosemary Cathcart, Sheelin Museum, Bellinaleck, Co Fermanagh

ACKNOWLEDGMENTS / BUÍOCHAS

In compiling this book, numerous secondary sources relating to the history of lace patrons and co-operatives were researched. Oral accounts were collected from the older crochet workers at lace storytelling nights since 1990, as part of the *Cassandra Hand Summer School of Clones Lace*. Lace-makers and their families were interviewed, as acknowledged. Family members of lace buyers also contributed. All projects are original.

The motifs and the patterns that I have transcribed here, come from an oral tradition, passed from mother to daughter for over 150 years. As such, you might find the patterns difficult to follow at times and I apologise for any difficulty you might have. As you become more experienced, the photos should overcome any problems.

I would like to thank all the lace-makers who have kept Clones lace alive for the next generation. These include Eileen Crudden, Anne Kelly, Alice Carey, Tessie Leonard, Tessie McMahon, Eileen Mc-Aleer, Raeleen Reavy, Annetta Hughes, Elizabeth Monahan and Nan Caulfield; Special thanks to Mariam Savage, who read and tested the patterns. Tess Daly has done a lot of work in the North Sligo area to keep Irish crochet alive and gave me valuable information and photographs for this book. I would also like to acknowledge those in the Roslea area, who we often call on when we have too many orders, requesting their assistance and who are also keeping crochet lace alive for another generation.

Thanks also to Mamo MacDonald, who first introduced me to Clones lace and to her son Brian, who gave me invaluable help and encouragement and read the manuscript. Mamo acted as chairperson of Clones Lace Guild for ten years. Mary Kelly served as our treasurer for almost 10 years, succeeding Eileen McAleer who filled this role when the Guild was originally established in 1988. Eileen remained as a committee member with Elizabeth Monahan, until 1999, when the marketing side of the Guild was taken over by Clones Development Association. All these people gave many hours of voluntary time to the revival and preservation of Clones lace.

I am indebted to the National Heritage Council for the financial assistance provided towards this publication. Warm thanks also to many individuals: Peadar Murnane, Maolíosa McCarthy, Sr Mona Lally, Cynthia Stewart, Pilip Ó Mórdha, George Knight, Esther Gray, Bernie Sheridan, Deborah Dawson, Mario Corrigan of Newbridge Library, county Kildare, Eileen France of Cork Textile Network, Tommy and Brigid Sheils, Miriam Moore, Terry O'Driscoll and the staff of the John Matthews Enterprise Centre and the Canal Stores, Clones. My lace-making students – Rosarii, Lily, Maura, Breda, Helena, Bridie, Alice, Josie and Ann – have been trying out and correcting my patterns for years. Jean Ness was an invaluable help in relation to the US sizes of the hooks and threads and in encouraging me to keep at this project!

Buíochas fosta do Glór na nGael agus Fás, a thug tacaíocht fostaíochta dom agus cuid den leabhar a scríobh agam – Bernie Nic Mhathúna ach go hairithe.

Tá mé thar a bheith buíoch as mo chlann – m'iníonacha Máiréad, Áine agus Cáit, mo dheirfiúr Aoibheann, a fearchéile Deaglán agus a gclann; mo dhearthaireacha Tarlach, Séamus agus a gclainn. Buíochas mór do Phat a chuidigh liom leis na páistí go minic, nuair a bhí mé faoi bhrú leis an leabhar seo a chríochnú.

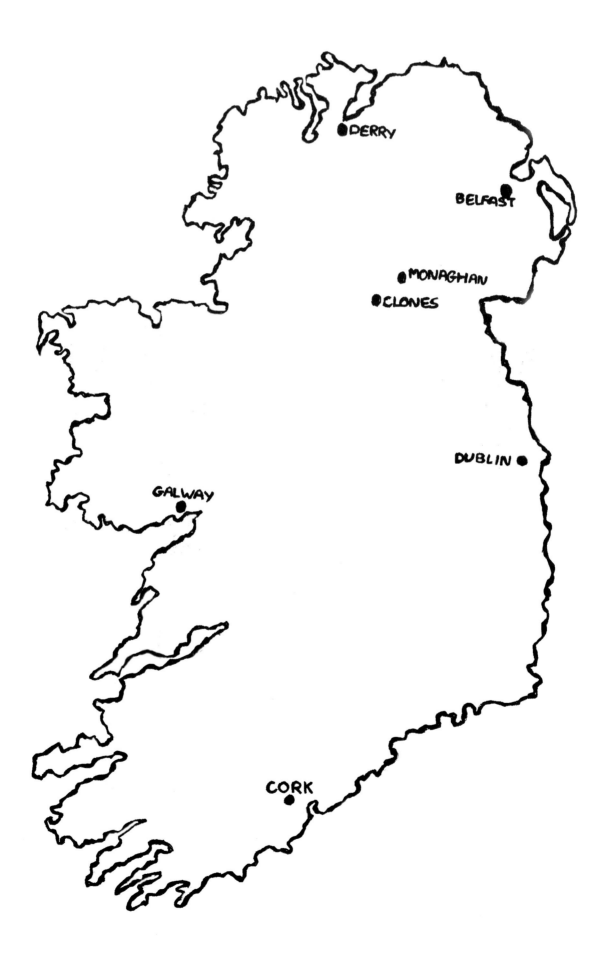

DERRY

BELFAST

MONAGHAN

CLONES

DUBLIN

GALWAY

CORK

Réamhrá

Tháinig Lása Chluain Eois ar an saol in 1847. Bhunaigh Cassandra Hand, bean Mhinistéir, mar scéim iar-Ghórta é, i ndiaidh a tháinig sí go Chluain Eois agus an Górta faoi lánsheol. Thug sí cúireadh do mhúinteoirí chróise ó 'Teach Thornton', Chill Dara a bhí oillte ag Bean Uí Roberts, teacht go Chluain Eois chun chróise Éireannach a theagasc. Bhí sé bunaithe ar Lása an Iodail – Lása shnáthaide.

Bhí án-suim ag muintir an limistéir ann agus bhí thart faoi achán chlann in ann é a dhéanamh roimh i bhfád. Ar ndoigh, bhí 1500 duine á dheanamh ins na 1850s. Ba ghnách leis na daoine siúl na mílte ó na limistéir tuaithe i bhFear Mánach agus Múineachán chun é a dhíol chuig na ceannaitheoirí ar lá mhargadh Chluain Eois gach seachtaine. Rinneadh ó'n líon, chadás, agus síoda é. Cúireadh le líon chun éadaí bhóird a dhéanamh fosta. Díoladh chuig an Ríshlíocht agus na hardaicme ar fud an domhain é.

Rinne na céirdithe blúsaí, coiléirí agus gúnaí ina dtithe féin. Ar an bharr sin, cúireadh an t-ainm 'cottage craftworkers' orthu. Bhí dhá shaghas lása ann, mar a bhí an cineál 'bhláthúil' agus 'na mín chearnóga'. Rinneadh ó shnaidhm le crúcaí án-mhín an dá chineál acu, ach baineadh usáid ó shnaidhm pháca an saghas bhláthúil, chun chuma thiúbh a chúr air. Níl a léitheid de chrúcaí agus de shnaidhm le fáil anois. Bhí cuma án-dathúil air agus rinneadh a mhacasamhail de ar fud an domhain, ach théipeadh ar an ardchéim de mhínchróise seo a ath-athrú. Níl morán daoine a dhéanamh anois ins an cheantar – idir seachtar agus fiche duine. Athbhunaíodh comharchumann lása in 1988 chun an lása a thabhairt ar áis ar an saol. Tá án-suim ag daoine chun é a fhoghlaim mar chaitheamh aimsire agus bíonn Scoilsamhradh Lása Chluain Eois ann achán bhliain.

Is cuid luachmhar d'oidhreacht na nGael é. Go maire sé i bhfád!

Foreword

Clones lace is an Irish Crochet lace, named after the town where it was marketed, developing its own character over nearly 150 years. Cassandra Hand, wife of the local Church of Ireland minister introduced it as a famine relief scheme to this small drumlin region of west Monaghan and south-east Fermanagh in 1847. Within a short period, nearly every family in the area was involved in the production of crochet lace, supplying markets in Dublin, London, Paris, Rome and New York. Clones soon became the most important centre of crochet lace-making in the north of Ireland, while Cork was the leading centre in the south.

Irish Crochet lace originally derived from specimens of Venetian rose point, first brought to Ireland in the 1830s by the Ursuline nuns in Blackrock, Cork from France. Indeed, the crochet lace that developed in Cork is very distinctive.[1] It comprises very large motifs, joined by thick bars, which are made up of double crochets stitched over foundation chains. There are varying accounts of between 12,000 and 20,000 girls being employed in its production from 1847. Mrs Meredith was the patron of the Adelaide school for crochet in Cork, which became a depot where lace was received and sold.[2]

In 1847, Mrs Roberts of 'Thornton' House, in county Kildare, having first unsuccessfully trained local people to knit woollen jackets as a famine relief scheme, trained a group of Irish crochet teachers. Cassandra Hand subsequently invited one of these young teachers to Clones, county Monaghan. The people of Clones were attracted by the use of a crochet hook, which gave the same effect as a sewing needle in a fraction of the time, recreating beautiful ornate floral work. Coupled with Cassandra's business ability and the talent and aptitude of the people in learning the craft, crochet very soon became associated with this drumlin region.

Crochet lace proved very popular throughout Ireland and lace-making teachers travelled to impoverished communities all over Ireland, acting as missionaries for the craft on behalf of the Congested Districts Board in the final years of the nineteenth century. By then regional variations had developed. In the nineteenth century, there were several types of Clones lace. In his account of 'Irish lace', published in 1886–8, Ben Lindsey names five types of Irish crochet:

> Plain crochet (made in one piece, which is the simplest and most common type of Irish crochet) was made in Cork (and throughout Ireland). The four other crochets were made in Clones and elsewhere: Jesuit Church crochet, Spanish crochet, Venetian crochet, and Greek crochet.

Today there are two types – the floral corded and the fine trellis rose and shamrock work. The lace-makers who, in the nineteenth century, made this 'coarse', or corded floral work, developed motifs of shamrocks, ferns, thistles, wild roses, lilies, marigolds, cartwheels and whitewash brushes.[3] These motifs, which represented the flowers of the countryside around them, were made with extremely fine thread and equally fine crochet hooks, using thicker packing cord to edge and define the motif, giving it a 'coarse' appearance. They also imitated the vine and grape motifs, which were used in all handwork and stonework in the nineteenth century and are common to the other laces of Ireland. The grape and vine are carved on headstones in local cemeteries of the period and embellished the embroidery on Church vestments. It is probable that, in Clones lace, they were intended to represent the Eucharist. Thelma Goldring has an interesting interpretation: that they were retained as a reminder of the Italian roots of the lace.[4] I would say that though both interpretations are true, it is more probable that the lace-makers just liked the grape and vine motifs.

Most families had their own secret and closely guarded motifs. The family nickname often reflected the motif with which the family was associated, such as the 'Lily Quigleys' or the 'Rosie McMahons'. When neighbours entered a house unexpectedly, the lace was hidden from view.[5] Their special motif was the basis of a family's income. Many motifs have gone to the grave due to this secrecy, although pattern makers examined finished pieces in the USA and England and transcribed them in Irish crochet publications.[6] Crochet workers delighted in creating new filling stitches, embellishments and motifs, as these would bring them a better income.

The Clones knot was the stitch often used to join the motifs in special pieces, though the picot filling stitch was more common. This distinctive knot was a ball made by flicking the hook 10–12 times left and right around the thread. Thousands of such 'rolled dots', as they are called in Fermanagh, filled a garment of lace, joining the motifs. They also developed the less common shamrock Clones knot, in which three Clones knots were joined together. In this 'freeform' corded crochet the motifs, or flowers, were joined with a mesh of chains and picots, or Clones knots, in a random way. A good designer could show her talents, creating beautiful blouses, collars and dresses. This floral work is based on even finer and painstaking needlepoint Venetian lace, which is still made on the island of Burano, off the city of Venice.

Fine trellis work became more fashionable at the turn of the twentieth century – fine rose and shamrock centres joined in squares. Rosie Mohan, now in her nineties, made the 'fine work' all her life, whereas her mother crocheted the 'coarse work'.[7] When Clones people think of Clones lace now, they think of these fine squares rather than the corded, or floral work, as this is what they remember being done in their own childhood homes by their mothers or grandmothers. This fine trellis work was in fact made throughout Ireland.[8] It is still made in the Clones and Roslea area and many distinguish it as 'Irish crochet'. In the past the shamrock, rose, thistle and leek motifs at the centre of these squares represented the national emblems of Ireland, England, Scotland and Wales. Today the rose and sham-

Máire Treanor crocheting

rock are still common centre motifs in Irish crochet squares. A few crochet workers kept this beautiful fine trellis work alive as a cottage industry in Fermanagh, edging linen handkerchiefs (hankies) and supplying linen merchants in Portadown and Belfast, who continue to export them all over the world. They also crochet edge and insert crochet squares to linen tableware. These workers also make table centres and collars, supplying the Ulster Canal Stores in Clones, which is now the showcase for Clones lace. Crocheted blouses usually feature both types of lace and are still, in 2002, made for special commissioned orders.

To crochet enthusiasts throughout the world, modern Irish crochet is made with a thicker thread, while table centres or collars are made in one piece and follow a pattern. Motifs used today are limited and don't involve packing cord. Although thread, rather than cord or wool is still used, it is much simpler to make than traditional fine Irish crochet lace. Clones lace retains floral nineteenth-century features that have now disappeared as Irish crochet was simplified and developed as a pastime!

In this publication, the terms 'lace-making' and 'crocheting' are inter-changeable, the latter term being used locally.

Clones lace Christening bonnet worn by Nancy Callanan's grandchild in 2000, USA

Christening booties and collar, crocheted by Mariam Savage, 2000

I first made this Christening outfit in 1990 for my second daughter Áine [left], with a lace bonnet, a lace band on the waist, a lace collar, cuffs and lace edging around the skirt.[9] This outfit was photographed for **Victoria USA** *in spring 1993 and led to a lot of new orders. It is my first Christening robe. I added lace to the front panel for the second baby, my godchild, Seán Ryan McCaffrey in 1991. Finally I made the sleeves, bodice and a 2" panel around the bottom skirt for my third child, Cáit [right] in 1992.*

An Irish Vine Garden by Máire Treanor, 2001

THE STORY OF CLONES LACE

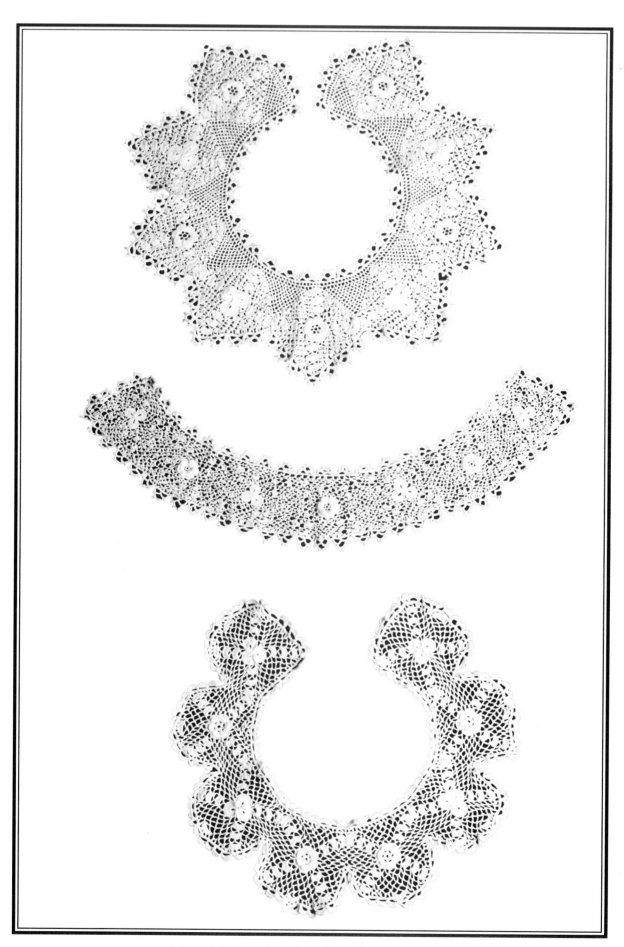

Various styles of Irish crochet collars, all made in this area

14

Clones lace has been a part of a way of life of the south-east Fermanagh and west Monaghan area since the famine period of 1847. Women and children made it to supplement a farming or an urban income, keeping ongoing famine and extreme poverty away and it often earned a ticket to a new life in the United States of America. Clones was the market town for crochet lace in this area. Interested and charitable people with connections in high society became patronesses for it, finding markets among wealthy aristocrats and royalty throughout the world at a time when one's position in society was very important. By the 1850s, almost all households in this small area crocheted, supplying markets in the fashionable cities of the world. At the turn of the twentieth century, when the co-operative movement had nationally replaced patronage, Clones was the most important centre of crochet lace-making in the north of Ireland, with Cork the leading centre of the south. Today, in the twenty-first century, people throughout the world learn Clones lace / Irish crochet as a relaxing and enjoyable craft hobby, though it is still commercially made in the west Monaghan and south Fermanagh areas of Ireland.

Cassandra Hand, nee More Molyneaux, first introduced crochet lace-making to Clones. The wife of a Church of Ireland minister (Reverend Thomas Hand), she travelled to Clones from England, when her husband was appointed rector to the parish in September 1847. The population of Clones poor law union was approximately 44,000 in 1846.[10] This was at the height of the Great Irish Famine, when thousands of people in this small area died from starvation and disease, while many more left on 'famine ships' to North America, Scotland, England, Australia and New Zealand. By 1851, the population of Clones poor law union had fallen to approximately 27,000![11] In fact, this area was one of those worst effected by the famine.

Life in Clones contrasted sharply to Cassandra's upbringing in her native Losely Park in Surrey. The Hands settled in the impressive rectory at Bishopscourt, on the outskirts of Clones. Having tried unsuccessfully to teach crochet making in England, she was moved by the extreme poverty in and around her adopted town and decided to promote crochet as a famine relief measure. In 1847, a teacher was brought to the town who had been trained by Mrs Roberts of 'Thornton' House in county Kildare, specialising in crochet, which had developed from the needlepoint lace.

Cassandra Hand – reproduced from a copy of the Clones Parish Bazaar *magazine, 1906*

SPRIGGING IN CLONES IN PRE-FAMINE PERIOD

The women of the Clones hinterland were very talented with their hands. Flax spinning into linen had been a very successful industry in the Clones area from late seventeenth century. When the flax crop began to fail in 1815, Nicholas Ellis, a local land agent, under the patronage of the Lennard Estate, strove to introduce a muslin-worked embroidery, bringing teachers from Ayrshire, Scotland, in the period 1829–1846.[12] The sprigging industry developed between 1839 and 1846, but seems to have died out as a distinct craft during the famine years, although it was later used as an embellishment on crocheted collars and tableware in the post-famine period.[13]

Antique Sampler, used by women, who couldn't read patterns, in nineteenth century – in the Sheelin Museum, Bellinaleck, county Fermanagh

MADEMOISELLE RIEGO DE LA BRANCHARDIERE

Mrs Roberts and Cassandra Hand used the crochet pattern books of Mademoiselle Riego de la Branchardiere as teaching aids. Mlle Riego, whose books inspired crochet workers everywhere, was born in England to a father of Franco-Spanish nobility and an Irish mother in 1820. She discovered that Spanish needle lace, which was similar in appearance to the exquisite Venetian needlepoint lace, could be adapted to the crochet hook and was much faster. A seven-inch piece of lace could be crocheted in about twenty hours, whereas the same piece would take at least 200 hours to sew with a needle.

Being keen to make her skills widely known, between 1844 and 1886, Mlle Riego published a series of books and periodicals of patterns and instructions. As she had Irish roots, Mlle Riego was anxious to personally assist the poor of Ireland and bequeathed a large sum of money to the Commissioners of Charitable Donations and Bequests to improve and encourage crochet lace-making in Ireland.[14] This grant was also used to train girls in art design for other Irish laces. Although Mlle Riego's pattern books were undoubtedly of great assistance to crochet workers, the Ursuline nuns in Cork must also be given credit for introducing crochet lace-making skills to the south of Ireland in the 1830s.

Cassandra opened a lace-making school in the rectory, now Bishopscourt. The people of Clones were keen to learn the craft and as Cassandra Hand later remarked, 'the flax spinning and sewing (linen embroidery) tradition gave the women an aptitude for handwork, making their fingers very nimble'. Clones lace was inexpensive to make compared to many other Irish laces, which required an expensive base material or net. The ball of thread crocheted a lot of lace and the hook could be filed out of a sewing needle and pushed into a wooden handle that was retained when the hook needed replacing. It was a very welcome industry for people who had suffered the ravages of famine. As they were generally illiterate, Cassandra, along with her Kildare teacher, passed on Mlle Riego's instructions orally and the crochet workers learned the various motifs from sample books. There are many local anecdotal accounts of classes being held at the rectory.[15]

> The workers in the district claim that women – and men – to the number of 1500, hurried from town and mountain in the first seven years after the Hands' arrival to learn the new designs that made Clones crochet sell at good prices …[16] The spinning and flowering industries carried on in the area may have made them neat-fingered …[17]

16

CROCHET LACE SCHOOLS

Lace schools became a feature of life in the south Ulster region as early as 1848. The early 1850s found schools with an emphasis on craft training in the Clones area. The authorities were hesitant in their reaction to this development, worried by the impact they were having on general education. A report to the Commission on Endowed Schools in Ireland by William Dwyer Ferguson, Assistant Commissioner, dated 2 June 1856, illustrates this point. Describing a lace school established in Clogh, county Fermanagh, he wrote:

> Both the master and resident curate stated that the establishment of crochet-work schools in the neighbourhood had seriously hindered the attendance of female children. I have heard this complaint repeatedly made through out the parish and I think it is a subject worthy of attention. These crochet-work schools are, in most instances, patronised by the clergymen of the parish; and though, no doubt, most valuable in affording industrial education, should not be made to preclude entirely all opportunity of a literary and religious education.

The women of Clones and its hinterland adapted Italian lace to their own life experience, replacing the ornate Italian flowers with those that they saw around them. They quickly became very skilled, displaying a talent for crochet work, industry and innovation. Cassandra managed the business, showing great aptitude. As the wife of a Church of Ireland minister, she had a strong religious fervour. She also had a very liberal attitude, which made her unpopular with the elders of her church. With her share of the proceeds from the lace industry, she had a school built, under the auspices of the Church of Ireland, for females and infants in Clones.[18] She also (and more controversially) bequeathed an organ to the Church of Ireland in the town at a time when Church music was frowned upon. The Church Vestry forbade it to be played for many years. In 1854, when she found that the management of the lace-making industry was taking up too much of her time, Cassandra tried to step down from her position, but the lace-makers made her a presentation of a Belleek china vase and begged her to continue as their manager. Their appeals were successful and she continued to manage the lace industry very successfully until her death, fourteen years later. She is buried in the picturesque churchyard at Clogh,

Female and Infant National School, Cara Street, Clones, built with Cassandra's proceeds of lace money

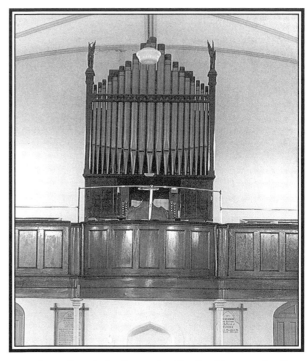

Organ bought by Cassandra Hand, with proceeds of lace money for the Church of Ireland, the Diamond, Clones

Church of Ireland, Clogh, outside Roslea, Co. Fermanagh, five miles from Clones, where Cassandra and her husband, Rev. Thomas Hand are buried

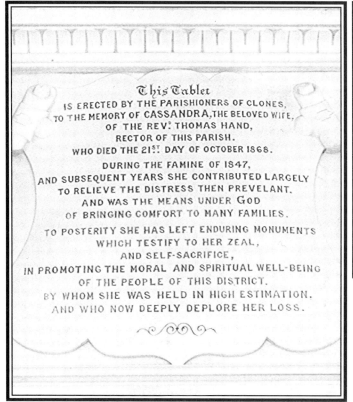

This Tablet
IS ERECTED BY THE PARISHIONERS OF CLONES,
TO THE MEMORY OF CASSANDRA, THE BELOVED WIFE,
OF THE REV! THOMAS HAND,
RECTOR OF THIS PARISH.
WHO DIED THE 21ST DAY OF OCTOBER 1868.

DURING THE FAMINE OF 1847,
AND SUBSEQUENT YEARS SHE CONTRIBUTED LARGELY
TO RELIEVE THE DISTRESS THEN PREVELANT,
AND WAS THE MEANS UNDER GOD
OF BRINGING COMFORT TO MANY FAMILIES.

TO POSTERITY SHE HAS LEFT ENDURING MONUMENTS
WHICH TESTIFY TO HER ZEAL,
AND SELF-SACRIFICE,
IN PROMOTING THE MORAL AND SPIRITUAL WELL-BEING
OF THE PEOPLE OF THIS DISTRICT.
BY WHOM SHE WAS HELD IN HIGH ESTIMATION,
AND WHO NOW DEEPLY DEPLORE HER LOSS.

The Rectory, later named Bishopcourt, on the outskirts of Clones, where the Hands lived – and where Cassandra gave the first classes in Clones lace[19]

Tablet in Church of Ireland, the Diamond, Clones

near Roslea, county Fermanagh.

Following her death in 1868, there was no effective management structure to replace Cassandra Hand and standards began to decline. Although Cassandra had employed a designer before she died, the work was so plentiful that it was often rushed and 'shoddily'-finished lace was submitted for sale. Lace-makers, who were neither particularly gifted nor well trained, crocheted to fill the many orders. This trend led to complaints and to buyers not wishing to re-order. Inferior work flooded the market, spoiling the craft for everyone. Handmade crochet became less attractive to its traditionally wealthy buyers at a time when cheaper machine lace from Nottingham in England and from Switzerland was becoming popular. The economic problems caused by the Franco-Prussian War made handcrocheted lace less popular. Beyond the immediate problems faced by lace-makers, the Irish rural economy, as a whole, was in serious trouble during this period and famine again threatened. The demand for Clones crochet lace slumped.

Revival in the Late Nineteenth Century

Due to the efforts of Isabel Madden, of Springrove Manor in Roslea and Lady Aberdeen, wife of the Viceroy in Dublin, Clones lace became popular once more in the 1890s. Lady Aberdeen was a very active patroness of all the Irish laces. Her husband was Viceroy in Dublin from 1886 to 1893 and again from 1906 to 1915. In 1893, maintaining her interest in Irish laces, Lady Aberdeen brought forty lace-makers to the Chicago World Fair. They returned with profits of £5,000. Isabel Madden procured an order for a dress worn by a Princess May in the early part of the twentieth century. The names of seventeen workers from the south Fermanagh area were given as those who worked on this dress in the *Impartial Reporter*.[20] Silk rather than cotton or linen thread was used in the work.

They also organised the Victorian Exhibition in London. 'Blousy Bell', as Lady Aberdeen was nicknamed, organised Society Lace Balls in Dublin, where each person was expected to wear a garment of Irish lace. The men wore jabots with their evening shirts, the women everything from blouses to bodices to cuffs, parasol covers, trimmings, dress fronts and even whole dresses. These social occasions had the intended result of reawakening interest in hand-made lace, thus leading to more orders for the lace-makers. Lady Aberdeen maintained an interest in Irish lace and remained as president of the Irish Industries Association.

Lady Aberdeen is remembered for a letter she wrote to the lace-makers, requesting them to take steps that would improve their health. As president of the Women's National Health Society, which had been founded in 1907, she was very aware of outbreaks of tuberculosis and other such diseases among the lace-makers. They were vulnerable due to their long-working hours, not getting enough fresh air and, indeed, not eating properly. In a letter to Isabel Madden, dated Vice Regal Lodge, Dublin, 21 May 1908, she wrote:

> I want you to be kind enough to convey my heartiest thanks to the lace workers who gathered at Clones yesterday – many of whom had walked into town from a considerable distance. In particular, I would like to ask you to tell Mrs Maguire how touched I was at the effort she made to be present.
>
> I had not time to touch upon the health question when speaking to the lace workers, but will you tell them that they can greatly help forward the Association by giving an example of what should be done in their homes.
>
> In order to keep the crochet clean they have to take great precautions, and this must naturally lead them to keep everything in connection with the house and themselves spotlessly clean. This is a great advantage in itself, but besides this, please ask them if they will not try this summer to keep their windows open more than they have ever done before and to do their work out of doors when they can do so, remembering that sedentary workers need as much fresh air as they can.
>
> Then, I fear that report says that they are apt to drink a great deal of stewed tea, and I would like to beg them for their own sakes and for the reputation of the health of the lace workers to make it a rule always to make their tea fresh whenever they require it, remembering what poison it is otherwise.
>
> And then there is one thing, when people oppose the making of lace and crochet, it is often urged that this occupation is very bad for the eyesight. Now I think that most crochet workers would deny this, but at the same time I fear that they are often apt to risk their eyesight by placing the lamp at night immediately in front of them, instead of to the left, from which side light should always come whether by day, or night for those who are making lace or embroidery, or indeed working in any way.
>
> I hope my friends will forgive me pressing home this upon them, but I want them very much to be leaders of the Women's Health Movement of Ireland as well as in the art of crochet making.
>
> When you let me know the number of the lace workers for whom you would like those pictures of myself, I will send them on to you.[21]

Many reports in the nineteenth and early twentieth century strongly advise lace-makers to sit in ventilated rooms and to get plenty of sunlight.

Isabel Madden played a key role locally in the revival of Clones lace and was keen to record the story of the craft in a letter to the local Fermanagh newspaper, the *Impartial Reporter*, circa 1898:

The Clones Lace or Guipure, which includes that of Rosslea and Aghadrumsee, has flourished for more than 50 years as the chief textile industry of the district. Established by Mrs Hand, of the Rectory, Clones, at a time when Ireland was slowly recovering from the ravages of the awful famine of 1847, it was the means of saving hundreds of people from utter destitution and of bringing comfort and happiness to every cottage home. After the death of this lamented lady, whose name is still a household word, the work was admirably carried on by Mr Ben Lindsey, under the South Kensington Art Society, from whom the beautiful floral designs, so much in vogue, were obtained. Mr Lindsey, being in touch with the continental markets, exported annually many thousands of pounds worth of Irish crochet. It was to be seen everywhere, from the remotest village in France, to the native huts in Jamaica.[22]

In 1893 the industry received a fresh impetus when the Irish Industries Association was organised, of which the Countess of Aberdeen kindly consented to become President. The Chicago Exhibition, better known as the 'World Fair' brought this beautiful lace into great prominence and notwithstanding the heavy duty which doubled its price, it found a ready sale. Lady Aberdeen continued to take a personal interest in the Clones lace, until other duties compelled her to resign the Presidency of the Irish Industries Association.

Her place has since been admirably filled by Her Excellency the Countess Cadogan, by whose efforts resulted the magnificent display of Irish manufacturers known as the Countess Cadagon's Textile Exhibition, held in Dublin in 1897, and visited by HRH the Duchess of York, who warmly expressed her admiration of the exquisite silk and cotton guipure exhibited at the Rosslea Manor Stall, which was the charge of Miss Mc-Mahon of Caraveetra. Miss Armstrong of Aghadrumsee, the same year, represented the industry during the six months of the Victorian Era Exhibition in London, under the personal supervision of the Marchioness of Londonderry, who took a special interest in the Irish workers ... successful trial pieces being paid for by the Branchardiere Bequest Fund. Mr Harry Biddle, of London, has from time to time lent valuable pieces of lace as Exhibition, visited their lodgings, invited them to tea at Londonderry House, and presented [them] with tickets for the Queen's Jubilee procession. Clones lace has been purchased by Her Majesty the Queen, HRH the Princess of Wales, the Ex-Empress of Russia and the Queen of Holland ... Foremost among the (lace buyers) I may mention Mr H. Lowe, Mrs Brady, and Mrs Kearns of Clones; Miss Gunn, Miss Maggie McMahon and Miss Armstrong, all who purchase the highest class of work, and who pay for it at market value. The Homestead, the organ of the Irish Industries, offers designs for crochet as models and by this means Venetian point, Mechlin, Spanish and Flanders laces have been reproduced by the crochet needle.

THE CO-OPERATIVE MOVEMENT

In the latter decades of the nineteenth century, various co-operative movements, such as the Irish Agricultural Organisation Society, were established which aided agricultural workers and lace-makers in particular throughout the west of Ireland. Leaders, such as Horace Plunkett recognised that there was a need to establish these co-operatives as protection against exploitation and bargaining and to counteract the weakness of the workers in demanding good prices for their work. There is evidence, though, that crochet fetched at least as good a price as some of the other more time-consuming laces.[23] With the advent of the co-operatives, the practice of patronage by the higher classes gradually became defunct.

THE LACE DEPOT

Irish crochet throughout the country was first marketed through the Lace Depot at 76 Grafton Street, Dublin, established by Ben Lindsey in the 1860s. Lindsey, an English lace-dealer found markets for Irish lace amongst the gentry and royalty all over Europe. Lady Aberdeen bought the Lace Depot when Lindsey died. In 1893, after her husband's transfer as Governor-General of Canada, she handed its management over to an unpaid board of directors whom she chose personally. Lace was sent from the Lace Depot to markets throughout the world. The Lace Depot was a non-profit-making organisation. As well as providing a sales outlet for the lace, it supplied designs to co-operative associations and schools of the Congested Districts Board. Its buyers travelled around the country buying the produce of the schools. It also paid the salary of lace teachers throughout the west of Ireland:

> The best period for Irish laces generally was between 1905–9, when the work done by Mr James Brenan and Alan S. Cole in encouraging the artistic education of teachers and workers alike was at last having results.[24]

In 1907, the annual earnings from the Lace Depot alone amounted to £100,000.

THE CONGESTED DISTRICTS BOARD EMPLOYS TEACHERS IN OTHER AREAS

In 1891, the British government, to aid the organisation of small industries in the congested districts of the west of Ireland, established the Congested District Board. Some of the best lace-makers from the Clones area were enticed by the Congested Districts Board to go as 'missionaries' to teach and spread the crochet lace-making tradition in various parts of the west of the country at the beginning of the twentieth century.

Liza Gunn from Derrylin, aunt of Elizabeth Monahan, went first to Bellmullet and then to Bruckless in the late 1890s where she founded a lace-making school. Bruckless developed as a great centre for Irish crochet and 'sprigging' work. Liza was the first person to amalgamate Irish crochet and sprigging on linen. According to Elizabeth, the women worked in a factory climate, with five groups – one group worked on the motifs, another on background joining stitches, a third on fine trellis centres and a fourth inserting the crochet into linen. A final group 'did up' or washed and starched the crochet. She also had girls 'sprigging' the corners of the hankies. Liza spent her life in Bruckless until 1951, when she retired back to Derrylin, county Fermanagh. Liza died in 1956.

Liza Gunn and her niece, Kate, in the 1940s

She brought her twelve-year old niece, Kate Gunn, a sister of Elizabeth, out of school in Derrylin to train and work with her. Kate stayed in Bruckless all her life. According to Elizabeth, Kate could crochet, but spent most of her time in the laundry. Liza travelled all over Donegal, teaching classes of Irish crochet. Elizabeth recalls that during the Second World War, linen was very scarce and Liza asked all her family to say novenas that she would get some linen. She used to travel up to Belfast, trying to get some. When Elizabeth Boyle researched Irish crochet in 1970, Teresa Gillespie, one of Liza's students had replaced Liza as manager the lace factory in Bruckless. Teresa who had been trained in the Dublin School of Art, managed the factory, renamed 'Teresa's Cottage',[25] for Gaeltarra Éireann, which had replaced the Congested Districts Board in 1920. Elizabeth Boyle's account in 1971 of Bruckless sets the scene:

> Mrs Gillespie now manages this factory for Gaeltarra Éireann and has as designer Mrs McCloskey, trained at the Dublin School of Art. She has 350 registered workers, 200 of these working full-time in the summer. Ninety per cent of the women are wives of small farmers or farmers themselves; the other ten per cent are young girls. All of them are active at home and some of them make embroidery and lace for two or three employers. Mrs Gillespie sends out the materials, which in the case of Miss Ritchie is Irish sewing cotton No. 60, and the women try to send in the finished work every two weeks, if they are not too busy milking or saving the hay. Not all of them live in county Donegal.[26]

Bruckless was the longest running lace school in the country!

Elizabeth Quigley of Roslea, aunt of Nan Caulfield, trained as a lace teacher with the Lace Depot in Dublin, founded her first crochet school in Blacksod Bay, on the coast of county Mayo. According to Nan, she was a very independent-minded woman. Nan often tells the story that Maud Gonne, a famous Irish revolutionary leader in the 1916 rebellion, travelled around the country, visiting the craft co-operatives. On hearing the price that these Mayo crochet workers were getting for their work from the Lace Depot, Maud let them know that it was fetching three and four times that price on the market in Dublin, London and Paris. Elizabeth decided to buy her own charcoal iron and washing materials to 'do-up' the group's work. She then sold it herself, rather than send it to the Dublin Lace Depot to be 'done-up' and sold. The group got a much better price for their work and she bought shares in Guinness brewery with the profit that she made! In the 1940s Elizabeth returned to Clones as Mrs Mullany, buying lace from other workers and selling it from her home in O'Neill Park.

In 1901, three Cosgrove sisters – Margaret, Catherine and Mary Jane were appointed by the Congested Districts Board to teach crochet in the west of Ireland. They left the Colehill area of south-east Fermanagh. Catherine went to Cliffoney in Sligo, Margaret went to Roundstone in Galway and Mary Jane (Jamie) to Renvyle in Mayo. (Margaret's descendants, the O'Dowds, have a prize winning

Cosgrove Sisters – Catherine, Margaret, and Mary Jane from Coleshill, county Fermanagh, who were appointed as instructors in the west of Ireland by the Congested Districts Board in 1901. Catherine went to Cliffoney, county Sligo, Margaret went to Roundstone, county Galway and Mary Jane went to Renvyle, county Mayo

seafood restaurant in Roundstone.) Tess (Teresa) Cosgrove, a niece, moved from Colehill to Cliffoney, where she learned the art of crochet making from her Aunt Kate (Rhatigan, nee Cosgrove). Tess' mother, Margaret Cosgrove nee McConnell was also an excellent crochet worker. Kate encouraged Tess to study Commercial Art in the National College of Art in Dublin, before returning to Cliffoney, where she married Seán Daly. In 1951, she resigned as an instructress with Gaeltarra Éireann and opened an Irish lace shop in Cliffoney, a popular tourist area.[27] She remembers that her aunt took orders for blouses and wedding tops from fashion shops in Sligo. A dressmaker would cut out a pattern in calico. Kate would pin motifs that she bought in from other lace-makers onto the pattern. A final lace-maker would fill around the motifs with the picot filling stitch.[28] The Clones knot was never used as a filling stitch in Sligo or Donegal. By the time Tess started her business in the 1950s, most of this old craft had died out and she specialised in tableware and hankies, with 'sprigged corners'. She had a lot of out-workers in Cliffoney and Ballintra, county Donegal.

All of these women were very independent, hard-working and career-minded women, who made a great impact and brought great employment to the rural areas where they settled.

Margaret Cosgrove neé McConnell, Lisnaskea, wearing her own Clones lace top circa 1900. Maggie's daughter, Tess went to live with her Aunt Catherine (Kate) in Cliffoney where she settled

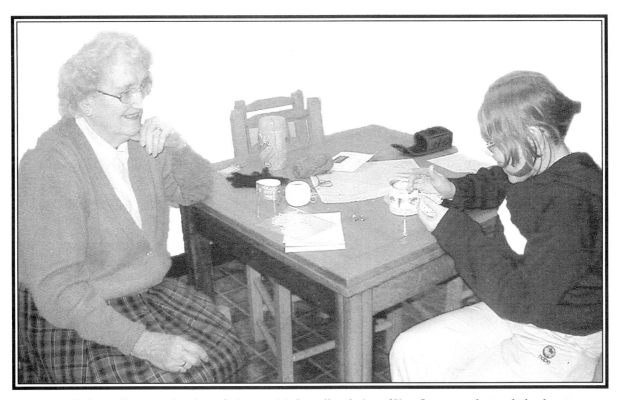

Tess Daly nee Cosgrove, daughter of Margaret McConnell and niece of Kate Cosgrove, who taught her how to crochet. She is passing on the craft to Ann Gallagher, showing her how to crochet a square in Cliffoney, county Sligo, in 1998

THE ROLE PLAYED BY THE SISTERS OF ST LOUIS

In January 1901, the sisters of the St Louis convent in Clones again took an active part in the lace industry, employing Miss Mulligan to teach crochet. According to the Clones Convent Annals, meetings of a Co-operative Lace Society were held in the convent school. Over the years more teachers were brought to the lace class; Miss Harris arrived in Clones from the School of Art in Cork in 1902 and was highly commended for her designs. At least one of the nuns, Sister Roche, was also employed to teach lace. The Department of Technical Instruction employed Mary Nagle from Cork to teach art and design in the convent and a grant towards instruction was obtained from the Technical Board for a few years, with over 200 girls employed at lace-making there in 1904. Prizes are recorded at the Monaghan County Show in 1903 for pillowslips, a crochet wool petticoat, a piece of crochet lace and a tea cosy. Indeed, the class won prizes at the county show up until 1914. By 1906 Clerys, a well-known department store in Dublin, was ordering large quantities of lace and clergymen were increasingly purchasing lace surplices. In 1908 a Diploma for Irish crochet was awarded from the *Daily Mail* Exhibition in the Municipal Building, London and in 1908 several first prizes were awarded at the Edinburgh Fine Arts Exhibition.[29]

LACE-MAKING IN SCHOOLS

In the Report of Agriculture and Manual Instruction (1909), Clones was noted for bad attendance:

> The county Monaghan ranks low in the school attendance statistics. The percentage of attendance to the number on the rolls of the National Schools in the county is the third lowest in Ireland, being only 58.1 percent. Some will suggest compulsory attendance. This is not always successful, for in the only town in this county, which has a school attendance committee – Clones – the percentage of attendance is the lowest of the towns.

The Committee of Agriculture and Manual Instruction sent instructors to schools throughout county Monaghan in an attempt to improve standards of lace-making, thereby increasing demand. Many of these girls were trained in Commercial Art classes in the Metropolitan School of Art in Dublin and in CDB teacher classes in South Kensington, London.[30]

By the turn of the twentieth century, nearly every family in the west Monaghan/south-east Fermanagh area was involved in the lace industry and by 1901, Clones was the most important centre for the production of crochet lace in Ireland. Virtually all female members of a family (and occasionally males!), young and old, had a role to play. Children as young as five could make 'buttonies' and 'hearts', while more experienced family members made the motifs. Sometimes the whole family was involved in completing an order; the children helped in making the motifs, while the mother finished off the piece, filling and edging it.[31] Children were often expected to make a number of heads before going to school and upon their return from school in the evening, they were allowed to skip up and down the lane once and then get back to their lace-making orders. They often stayed off school to finish an order.[32]

I discovered that my great-grandmother (who died in her late 80s in 1947) and two of her daughters crocheted centre pieces and crochet-edged linen hankies. They came from Aghnaglough, county Monaghan.[33] In a report by Henry Worsley, Inspector of National Schools in 1893 the school, which they attended is named in connection with Clones lace:

> A well-qualified teacher, Miss Tierney, is engaged at present teaching (Clones crochet lace) to seventeen girls in the convent where all the work is executed. The Clones crochet is taught in only one National School in the district, in Aghnaglough in the parish of Monaghan, having been recently introduced there.[34]

In some localities, children were given the choice to go to the 'learning' class, or the lace class. Annie Freeman of Drum, county Monaghan, opted to go to the lace class, as they would learn something that would earn them a living and also offered them the exciting chance to travel to Dublin for further training in design work![35] They might even become lace-making tutors. This gave them the chance to travel away to live in other counties, at a time when it took days to travel to counties at the opposite end of the country. A trip to the local town just fifteen miles away was considered a big occasion, requiring a very early start at dawn.

In the same article in the report of the Committee of Agriculture and Manual Instruction, 1909, already referred to, Theresa Leonard, lace instructor, wrote that the craft halted emigration among girls during periods when lace was in demand. Killeevan parish, a few miles outside Clones, is singled out as having benefited from improved standards:

> In the parish referred to, since the advent of instruction emigration has ceased, so far as girls are concerned and in other districts the class of article has considerably improved, with the result that the demands are good.

'You wouldn't go on your céilí without your crochet!'

After the potato famine, lace-making became a means of putting food on the table for many Irish families. During the many times of food shortage in the nineteenth century, it was a means of providing supplemental employment in areas where farming alone was not sufficient to keep a family out of the poorhouse. To protect their hands, lace-makers were generally exempt from manual farm duties. Herding of farm animals was permitted, however, as this could be combined with lace-work. In the Roslea area of county Fermanagh, Annie Cassidy always took her crochet with her while she herded the cattle.[36] Lace-making was a lucrative business for many and stories abound of farms being bought with the proceeds of 'crochet' money. Accordingly girl babies were more valued than baby boys, as they would become crochet workers and the crochet hook gave these women dignity. Roslea farmers were described as the 'worst in the country, as the men did the housework, while the women crocheted'![37] This reflected the fact that the small mixed farm economy of the region wasn't sufficient to feed a large family. Lace-making was part of the community. Women 'went on their céilí' to each other's houses and crocheted, while the men played a game of cards. As Tessie Leonard remarked 'You wouldn't go on your "céilí" without your crochet!'[38] Crochet lace-making was most popular in areas where the land was poor, as lace-money bought the groceries for the rural family. According to one veteran lace-maker, crochet workers had to keep their hands soft, with the exception of the left forefinger. It was burned brown to harden it against the crochet hook.

Fair Day in Clones

In the 1901 census, virtually every household in south Fermanagh put down crochet making and farming as their mode of livelihood. Rising at dawn once a week, they walked from Roslea, Aghadrumsee and other country areas once a month, to the fair at Clones to sell their crochet to buyers. Fair day was a great social event for the country people. There are lots of stories of women travelling to Clones on horse-drawn carts or by train, with the crochet on their laps. Women walked from daybreak from the more remote parts of the district. It was held once a week in most towns in Ireland. Farm animals were sold and goods such as tea and sugar that couldn't be grown on the farm were bought.

This account of another Monaghan fair day (in Ballybay) sets the atmosphere of the fair in the late nineteenth and early twentieth century:

> The town would be 'chock-a-block' with travelling shows of all descriptions: 'trick-or-the-loop' men, 'roulette stalls', 'wheel of fortune', 'dice', 'roll-em-in', 'three card trick' and 'pea in the thimble'. Confidence men would line the streets with their stalls. Musicians were many and varied: playing button key accordions, con-

Type of road that country people walked to the fair in Clones

certinas and an odd violin. The rare treat would be the itinerant uilleann piper. A strong man would pull a cart with a rope caught in his teeth and for an encore, might ask a man from the audience to tie him up with a chain and wager how quickly he might untie himself unaided. Occasionally, an elderly bearded man and his young daughter, both dressed in highland costume, would daringly dance the sword dance on crossed claymores. An enterprising showman would usually set up his swings and hobby horses on the vacant ground behind the market house and remain there from the loosening fair to the hiring fair. Ballad singers would render songs about politicians and other heroes and events and sell copies of their sheets around the town. One recalls the wonderful voice and banjo [playing] of Maggie Barry. 'Ere a song yourself, sir', would be their introduction. Of course, the pickpockets would have a field day![39]

In the Clones area, buyers in the local shops collected the out-workers' produce on fair day. Women met at Dernawilt Cross, about four miles from Clones, between Roslea and Donagh in county Fermanagh and went to town on a brake (a horse-drawn long open-topped carriage). They each had a basketful of lace and on their way to town, they discussed the prices they hoped to get for their collars or centre pieces. On their return, they compared what prices they had got – between two and three shillings for a centre or collar. Some would have added on a few pence to their price, to make their neighbour jealous. The following list gives an idea of how the lace-making money was spent on fair day:

> A woman brought in some lace made by her children to a shop, the proprietor of which was a lace agent in a small way. Her lace was valued at £1. Out of this she paid an account of 7s 6d for thread, and bought the following goods $^1/_2$ lb. of tea at 1s 4d, $^1/_2$ stone sugar at 1s 2d and a quart of whiskey at 5s. At another house in the town she paid an account of 3s 4d for hats for her daughters and had just 2s home out of her £1 worth of lace.

Thus, women returned from fair day with a cart filled with goods that they had bought with the proceeds of the lace-money. Other women walked from Cooneen, county Fermanagh, fourteen miles away to the fair.

THE BARTERING SYSTEM

In Clones, some of the crocheters were paid in cash, but most exchanged the crochet for other household goods such as sugar, tea and flour, or material to make clothes for the family. There are lots of harsh stories told about this 'bartering system'. Families depended on the lace to buy their household goods. Lily Mooney, whose mother Mary McGurk was one of the best crochet workers in the Clones area, remembers a story often recounted in her Aunt Brigid's family: Brigid Boylan, of Cara Street, sold her crochet to one of these 'buyers'. Having rushed to finish off her crochet, she sat up late at night over the previous weeks, so that she could get a goose for the Christmas dinner. On reaching the buyer's shop on Christmas Eve she discovered that the crochet paid off the grocery bill, but it didn't earn the family a goose!

BUYERS OF LACE

The *Clones Directory*, published in 1909, has a list of lace-manufacturers, or 'middle men', at that time. These included:

> Hugh Maguire, the Diamond; J Black, Newtownbutler Road; John Tummon, Erne Square; Miss McCarron, do; Philip Maguire, Fermanagh Street; Miss McMahon, do; Edward Brady, do; Hugh Gunn and Co., do; Miss Tierney, Pound Hill; Kirkpatrick Bros, Woods and Co., Fermanagh St; James Armstrong, do.

The 'middle' women or buyers serviced this cottage industry, employing staff to launder the lace and linen to prepare it for sale, as the out-workers often lived in very poor conditions, without running water. Some of the workers tried to keep it as clean as possible, rolling their lace work up in a sheet and putting it in the bed when they weren't working at it, to keep it clean. But, I have heard other stories of women sitting crocheting while the cat played with the ball of thread.

Margaret Jane McCaffrey, a fine lace-maker, was trained first as a laundry mistress and then as a buyer for the Hibernian Lace company, which was managed in Clones by the Tierney family. Their main office was in Dublin, but they had a large lace establishment in Fermanagh Street, Clones, with a lot of people working for them. Margaret's sister, Mary Ann, was also a fine lace-maker and also worked for the Tierneys. Both girls became instructors and, following training in Dublin, taught lace-making in the north of county Monaghan. Margaret travelled to Belfast and continued to sell Clones lace there. She employed two girls to launder the lace – one from Lisnaskea, the other from Ballybay. She had lace posted to her from the Clones area and sold it to the big shops, such as Robinson and Clevers in Belfast. She later married, staying in Belfast, but returned as Mrs Murnane to Ballybay in 1922. Her son, Peadar Murnane remembers that as a child he used to bounce on large sacks that were very soft. There were about twenty or thirty of these sacks in the barn at the back of the house. Then during the Second World War, his mother took out these sacks, revealing hundreds of squares of crochet lace, which she had bought while still in Belfast, and got to work. To join the pieces, she re-employed the women from the south Fermanagh area that she had worked with in the Hibernian Lace Company. She then sold everything from blouses to centres to American soldiers billeted in Ireland, who sent them home to their loved ones. Mrs Murnane bought the crochet squares and placed them on templates, which a final woman joined into blouses. Later, Irish couturiers with a world wide reputation in dress design, such as Sybil Connolly and Irene Gilbert, bought lace blouses and accessories from her. She continued to buy lace from workers in the south Fermanagh area until 1958. Margaret Jane Murnane died in 1961.

Peadar Murnane continued in the trade for a few years, driving around the countryside in a van. He remembers that one of his suppliers was Mrs McMahon of Derrylea, Scotstown.[40] She made ten pairs of gloves every month. He still had one of these beautiful fine pairs of gloves in an old suitcase that he produced. It was filled with dozens of clear plastic bags of carefully laundered crochet – crochet bows, squares and inserts for tray cloths and table cloths. His wife and daughter had a blouse each – keepsakes from another time, when the crochet business was a very lucrative income for this family and all the people that they employed. These included women such as Mrs Bannon of Corranney, Mary Jane McElgunn of Killyfoyle, Mrs Killen of Aghadrumsee. Mary Maguire edged hankies and made half a dozen pairs of gloves every month. Mrs Kelly of Dernawilt was one of the best crochet workers in the area. She made thirteen table mats, six small table centres and six large table centres every two months.

The following account of Rose Black, a well-known buyer on the Newtownbutler Road in Clones, was told to me by her great grandchildren, John and Mary Martin. Widowed young, with twelve children, Rose was a dressmaker by trade and made lace herself. As a means of rearing and educating her family, she started dealing in lace and became one of the better known 'middle women' in the town. Lace was often exchanged or 'bartered' for other goods that the women needed. According to local accounts, Mrs Black gave the workers lengths of material to make clothes for their family in exchange of their lace. Her company was known as the Clones Lace Depot (1907–1940s) and was operated from her home. The lace-makers brought the lace to her, entering through the back of the house, where she had a 'washroom' to launder it for sale.

Rose Black sold Clones lace onto traders who came to her and also through the Dublin Lace Depot. She taught her daughters her trade and they carried it with them throughout their lives. When Mary and John were telling me about their family, they jokingly referred to lace underwear that their Aunt Nancy had crocheted for them to wear as children. All of Rose's family became professionals – two were solicitors and one was a schoolteacher in the Clones area. All were educated on the money made from lace. Much of Rose Black's lace was made with silk thread, which she bought abroad and gave to her lace-makers.[41]

Before her retirement from business, Mamo MacDonald had a teashop and lace gallery in one of these buyers' shops; that of Hugh Gunn.[42] Originally from a lace-selling family in Fivemiletown, county Tyrone, he sent Clones lace to Willie Ahern, of Cobh, county Cork, one of whose friends was Michael Bowen, Mamo's grandfather! Mr Ahern sold all kinds of Irish lace 'by the baleful' to the ships that left for America from Cobh. Hugh's sisters of Fivemiletown were also involved in the lace-selling business, travelling around Roslea and Scotstown, collecting lace. When I first got to know her in the late 1980s, Tessie Leonard worked for the Gunn sisters. I remember Tessie crocheting edges onto table cloths that had drawn threads worked on them, by an old woman of ninety, in county Down.[43] The famous Cross of Malta had been worked in each corner. The Gunn sisters supplied the order. 'They were two very straight old ladies and never quibbled about the price that I asked for the work.' Tessie crocheted insets and edges to table linen, which they supplied. Other local crochet workers crocheted all sizes of table centres for them.

The McGorrys, who lived in the Diamond in Clones were well-known lace buyers between 1900 and the 1940s. Their daughter Eithne D'Arcy, started crocheting in the 1950s and subsequently wrote a book on the motifs used in Clones lace. They had workers as far as away as Ballybofey in Donegal, who sprigged corners to linen tableware and hankies for them. Kathleen Cassidy recently found an old box, belonging to her grandmother, Annie Freeman, a lace-maker from Drum, county Monaghan. Some packing cord was wrapped around a piece of paper. When Kathleen opened the paper, she found a beautifully hand-written letter in ink dated 1944, written by Mrs McGahern of Ballybofey, county Donegal, addressed to her lace buyer, Mrs McGorry, the Diamond, Clones.[44] This letter gives an insight into the lives of those who crocheted for the McGorrys.

Mary Kilcoyne was another buyer who had an Irish crochet shop in Fermanagh Street, the main street in Clones, until her death in 1970. According to her niece Olive Byrne, Mary stocked mainly handkerchiefs, traycloths, cheval sets, crochet collars, cuffs and bows. These articles were very popular as Christmas gifts and with the summer visitors to the town. The collars and bows were made up completely of crochet, while the tray cloths and tableware were Irish linen edged with crochet. Items made especially to order included linen and crochet supper cloths, luncheon sets, crochet blouses and Christening robes. Unlike many of the other buyers, she didn't partake in the 'bartering system' and paid the workers in cash as soon as they arrived with their work. Her crochet workers included Molly Maguire, who edged lawn linen hankies for her, calling each week for her supply of linen squares, and returning the following week with the finished hankies. Cassie O'Neill crocheted blouses for her. Both of these women were from just across the border in Aghadrumsee, county Fermanagh. Susan Sheils, another of her out-workers, was from Edergole between Scotstown and Redhills, county Cavan. She was an expert in joining crochet to linen, an art in itself. The workers brought in their lace unwashed, and Miss Kilcoyne (as she was known) laundered it. Olive recalled her aunt's secret recipe which she mixed to launder the crochet. It consisted of chloride of lime, washing soda and water in a bucket, which was stirred once a day, over a week, before being bottled. Some of it only needed to be washed to tighten up the stitches, while other work was brown with dirt when it came in, reflecting the living conditions of the various workers.[45]

Not all crochet workers went to Clones to sell their lace. There were also buyers in the country areas, mostly around Roslea. One of the better known of these was Sarah Martin, who according to Nan Caulfield 'looked under her glasses to examine the lace and pulled the crochet out and up to make sure there were no holes in it, nor bad thread used! She was a very tall, straight lady. She only bought crochet from the best workers in the area and gave them linen maniloves thread with which to crochet.' In the early part of the 1900s, she supervised and designed a dress made mostly by four sisters – Annie, Mary, Margaret, and Cathy Beggan. Mary Boyle, their cousin made most of the big flowers in it. According to research done by Mamo MacDonald, one of the 'Lily Quigleys' made all the lilies for this dress. They went to Sarah's house to crochet and Sarah modelled the dress at an exhibition in the RDS, Dublin. It was purchased on behalf of Queen Mary.[46] A daughter of one of Beggan sisters – Rosina Sweeney, still lives at Gortnawinney, two miles outside Clones. Now in her eighties, she has crocheted the fine rose and shamrock collars and centre pieces all her life.[47]

The 'flyer' Quigleys were also well-known sisters who collected crochet around the country areas. They would set out on bicycles in different directions from their home in Cooneen in the Sliabh Beagh mountains and ride around the countryside collecting motifs, table centres and hankies, which they took home to 'do up'. In the 1940s, a Miss Leonard similarly travelled around the homes of the workers in the country areas, collecting table mats, tray cloths, hankies, gloves and collars. Mrs Cunningham also bought lace around the south Fermanagh area. Mary Quigley of Crockada was another buyer in the Roslea area. The crochet workers in Roslea recently told me about women who used to buy the lace from their aunts and neighbours. They would go to a post office in another town with the crochet that they sent to America, just in case a local person might see the address of the store to which they were sending it in the USA and try to cut them out of business! The women took their crochet to Mass on Sunday and met the buyer, who bought their work at the gates after Mass!

Brigid Toal of Drumguill, Threemilehouse, county Monaghan was an agent for Harrods in London. Once a month, she rented a room in Hill Street, Monaghan. The lace-makers came into her with their pieces of work. She chose the best pieces that were of a high enough standard and would be in demand in London and gave them the going price for their work.[48]

Sarah Martin modelling this dress at the RDS in 1907. Local lore says that Queen Mary bought it as her coronation dress in the early 1900s.

'POINT D'IRLANDE'

The French fondly referred to Irish crochet as *Point d'Irlande*. James Brenan of the Crawford Municipal School of Art in Cork trained women in Limerick lace, Carrickmacross lace and Irish crochet lace design over three years. In 1902, he wrote:

I have been told by M. Lefébure that Irish crochet has a distinctive character which it is impossible to imitate on the continent: and that if the lace became really fashionable and proper attention was paid to the effects which might be produced in it by careful supervision, it was still possible to make it one of the leading and most attractive of laces.

The (crochet) work produced in different districts varies in character. That made in the south of Ireland is more open and contains larger forms than the northern crochet. The Clones lace is very beautiful [and] has a distinctive knotted filling, and is in my judgement capable of great improvement.[49]

PROTECTING THE MARKET FOR LACE

The French did, however, try unsuccessfully to imitate Irish crochet lace. At the turn of the twentieth century, Irish lace was made in Brittany, lace-makers being brought over from Ireland to teach their craft.[50] One Irish paper bemoaned the trend:

> The French mean a great deal when they refer to it in their own expressive and picturesque way as having been made by the 'fairy fingers' of the Irish peasant girls … It is certainly more flattering than profitable to Ireland to see that France now makes its own 'Irish lace', which by the way has nothing of Irish lace but the name … does not rise above the level of vulgar crochet-work; it is coarse and liable to stretch … The imitation is sold in the French market as bona-fide Irish lace … this cheap, vulgar imitation will inevitably render the Irish lace less popular on the French market. The poorest factory girl can now trim her Sunday dress with Irish lace made in France …
>
> Since over a year Irish lace is being made in Brittany. I have it on good authority that lace-makers were even brought over from Ireland to teach in schools established to run Irish lace-making on a large scale. In other parts of France there are similar concerns of which the output is less important. Slowly, perhaps, but surely, the undermining process is going on, and unless measures be taken to stem it, the Irish lace business will shortly be hurried along the road to ruin.[51]

They also reproduced machine-lace imitations of it.[52] Indeed, imitations of Irish crochet still 'flood' the market, as Mamo MacDonald remarked in 1993:

> We can't win … Generations ago, Irish missionaries travelled to Asia and taught the Taiwanese to do Irish crochet lace. Today, Taiwan actually exports lace to Dublin gift shops, where the shopkeepers tack it up on green backgrounds and sell it as 'Irish lace'. The work is not nearly as fine as Clones lace but it is cheaper and most tourists are happy enough to return home with anything bearing the name 'Irish lace'.[53]

MEN ALSO CROCHETED!

Despite the preference for lace-making among girls, men also crocheted, though most were happy enough to farm their smallholding and they often supported the women with their household and childminding duties. I remember one night, a local man called Siricus McPhilips came in and when he saw me working at my lace, scolded me for the way I was sitting under the wall light, with the work too close to my eyes. He said that he and his brother Raymond both crocheted when they were younger. Their mother had been a very good crochet worker. There was a man in the Roslea area, Francis James Sonna, who was well known as an expert crochet worker. His sisters were also good crochet workers. Ciarán Leonard, son of Tessie, told me that he made 'hearts' (the centre roses and shamrocks) for his mother's work when he was a boy. Ciarán and some of her other sons also made hooks out of sewing needles. Her only daughter, Louisa, crochets beautiful huge table centres. I was surprised to hear recently that another great local community organiser, Jim Flynn, used to crochet. He crocheted a First Communion dress for his niece and made a bedspread in thicker crochet. He had learned the art of crochet from his mother and sister.

'BURNHEEL CROCHETERS'

During the Second World War munitions factories, needing nimble fingers, lured young girls away from the quietness and security of the home. The atmosphere of the factory floor seemed much more exciting. Nan Caulfield recollects that those who remained at home were derogatorily nicknamed 'burnheel crocheters', reflecting the image of sitting by the fireside, while they crocheted! By this time, crocheting wasn't seen as a particularly 'with it' thing to be doing. Twenty years before that, it was seen as a way to travel to Dublin to study design, and then to teach it in various parts of the country.

CROCHET THREAD

Traditionally, Clones lace is usually made with white or ecru thread. Although ecru thread was available, it was often made ecru in the past by soaking it in tea.[54] Tessie Leonard told me that her Aunt Jane made black blouses in the 1930s and 1940s. Black thread is particularly hard to see when working with it, though. Coated cotton thread has been used locally since the Second World War, when the factory, which made maniloves linen thread, was air-bombed. It isn't as strong as the linen thread and doesn't have the same crisp feel. During the Second World War, thread became very scarce, with crochet workers reluctantly using single picots rather than double picots in their work.

The Clones knot used a lot of thread and this is probably one of the reasons why it died out, although at this time the art of doing corded motifs had been replaced by fine trellis work. Following the traditional ways, in the local guild we all use No. 40 fine cotton thread to make the motifs, or crochet the squares and we use a finer No. 50 to fill in between the motifs. Nan Caulfield suggested we use a finer thread to fill in the piece, using thicker thread for the edging and the motifs.[55] At the turn of the century, 200-gauge thread would have been used, with equally fine hooks. Neither the thread nor the hooks are available now, with mercerised thread becoming popular in the 1960s. Some people like to use this mercerised thread, which is stronger, although the cotton thread is softer. Silk thread was often used at the turn of the century and is still used occasionally, but it is thick and more difficult with which to crochet. Crochet workers use various colours of thread, according to fashion trends, but the traditional colours of white and ecru are timeless.

CROCHET HOOKS

When crochet lace-making was first introduced in 1847, there are reports of hooks being made out of wire. Later on, as it developed into an industry, hooks were purchased in packs of ten in the shops in Clones, in the same way as sewing needles would be bought. During the world wars, when it became impossible to buy the steel hooks, local people reverted to making the old 'famine hooks' out of sewing needles. John Joe McElroy from Selloo Post Office, near Scotstown in county Monaghan, was a well known hook-maker. John Joe was a clock-maker and had a lot of suitable tools for making the hooks. He used some of his clock-making tools to bend the bottom end of the sewing needle, making the hook. All the older Fermanagh crochet workers that I know use John Joe's hooks. The crochet worker inserted them into a cane handle, which she kept. Some crochet workers, such as Nan Caulfield, wrapped soft bailing cord or wool around the handle, so as to make it soft on the hands. She heated the base of the hook off the stove fire and then pushed it in, so that the heat firmed it. In other households, the piece of cane was put into a 'pot of boiling spuds, to soften it and then the hook was pushed into it.' I have also seen handles made from a ruler for the shaft, with the middle, where it was held, worn and smooth, due to long use over many years.

Hugh Doran recalls as a child watching his grandmother, Bridget McGinnity, crocheting. They

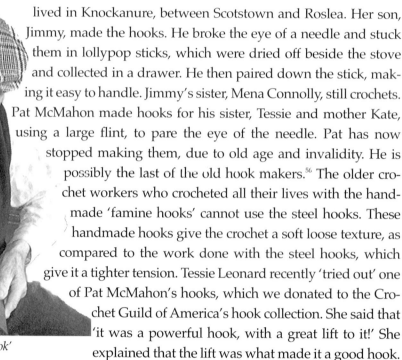

lived in Knockanure, between Scotstown and Roslea. Her son, Jimmy, made the hooks. He broke the eye of a needle and stuck them in lollypop sticks, which were dried off beside the stove and collected in a drawer. He then paired down the stick, making it easy to handle. Jimmy's sister, Mena Connolly, still crochets. Pat McMahon made hooks for his sister, Tessie and mother Kate, using a large flint, to pare the eye of the needle. Pat has now stopped making them, due to old age and invalidity. He is possibly the last of the old hook makers.[56] The older crochet workers who crocheted all their lives with the handmade 'famine hooks' cannot use the steel hooks. These handmade hooks give the crochet a soft loose texture, as compared to the work done with the steel hooks, which give it a tighter tension. Tessie Leonard recently 'tried out' one of Pat McMahon's hooks, which we donated to the Crochet Guild of America's hook collection. She said that 'it was a powerful hook, with a great lift to it!' She explained that the lift was what made it a good hook.

Pat McMahon 1996, making 'famine hook'

Those, like me, who learned with the steel hooks, cannot use the 'famine hooks'. I first heard them called famine hooks by Mary Coleman, President of the Guild of Irish Lace-makers. I have seen very beautiful ivory and ornate hooks, which women in America collect. Nancy Nehring of the South Bay Crochet Chapter, USA, is an authority on all types of hooks and was fascinated by the simplicity of the Irish handmade hooks. The Clones 'famine hooks' are very ordinary and used looking. As Nancy remarked, 'they have a great story to tell!'

EYESIGHT

The crochet workers often sat up late at night finishing orders by the light of oil lamps. I have often heard stories of people going blind and continuing to crochet. Nan Caulfield tells stories of blind men crocheting. According to Alice Connolly, Mary Beggan always said that 'you knew if you were doing the right thing by the feel of it.' The older crochet workers cannot do a motif that entails working around the packing cord all the time, such as in the vine leaf, 'because of all that liftin', as it means that 'you have to concentrate and look at what you're doing all the time.' When crocheting, it is important not to stare into your work. Try to hold it at your waist, sitting straight, with the light behind you. Lady Aberdeen's instructions are still as relevant today as they were then.

CROCHET WORK – A LIVING TRADITION

There were a lot of crochet workers in the Clones area, whose families are still alive. Mary Ellen Toye lived in the same terrace as me, though she was in her eighties and had stopped crocheting when I became interested in Clones lace.

Brigid McCabe's mother, Josephine McCaul was a great crochet worker, as was her mother, Mary McCaul. Brigid tells me that nearly every family crocheted in Clones when she was young. She proudly reflects that Mary's mother was one of the first generation of lace-makers in Clones. Brigid's mother, as a child, carried a basketful of lace to the buyer in Clones and returned with a sovereign. The money wasn't sufficient for the weeks of work that she spent. Not only had she crocheted the pieces, but it had also taken days to launder them. Four sisters crocheted – Mary, Maggie, Babs and Frances

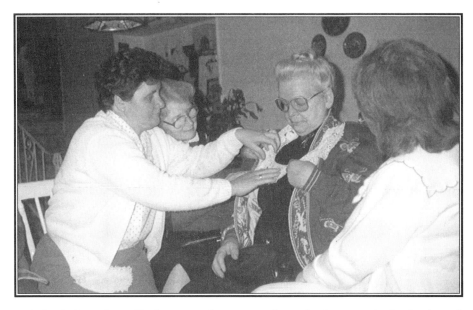

Breda Bohan admiring Mary Ellen Toye's collar at Cassandra Hand Summer School, 1991

McCaul. Brigid recalls them washing, stretching the lace out in the backyard, and starching it. Brigid's sister, Katie McGuigan can still crochet, when called upon. Brigid, though she didn't take up lace-making, is well known in Clones as a dressmaker. Two sisters, Tess and Agnes Slowey from Carra-veetra were great crochet workers up until their death. Their niece, also Tess Slowey, told me that they made tray cloths and table centres. Tess spent her life nursing in Boston, and retired home to live with her sister Agnes. They made lace for the big stores in Dublin. Agnes died, aged 78, in 1966. Tess lived on in Millbrook in Clones, continuing to crochet until 1978 when she died at the age of 83. In 1968 May Lyttle, from Golanduff, Clones and formerly of Killyfoyle, Roslea made a large linen and Clones lace table centre as a wedding present for Maeve and Billy Vance.

Large centre piece made by May Lyttle, Golanduff Clones, in 1968

Clones is full of old pieces, many of which are precious family heirlooms.[57] They are usually crocheted in fine trellis work. It is unusual to see the older motifs and Clones knot in a piece.

In this era, Maggie Lavery did a lot of crochet in the area. She also taught it. Mrs Quaile, originally from Scotland, made beautiful blouses up until the 1960s.[58] Vera Reilly, her sister Annie Kerr, Rosina Sweeney and Elizabeth Monahan taught Clones lace to the local branch of the Irish Countrywoman's Association, which did a lot of work in the preservation of Clones lace over the years, before the modern Clones Lace Guild was established.[59] I remember talking to a Roslea woman, Cassie McElroy in 1990,

at a lace exhibition in Roslea. The crochet workers of Roslea had organised a crochet lace display as part of our first *Cassandra Hand Summer School*. At the age of 85, she had six orders for blouses. It took her six months to do one! She died at 90, in 1995. Her daughter Sarah Mulligan, still crochets with the Roslea Lace Guild.

Cassie McElroy in Roslea 1990

EMIGRANTS WHO MADE IRISH CROCHET

Many emigrants brought fine crochet skills with them to their new country when they left Ireland and they did some magnificent work. They did not continue to do it as a chore for money, as they would have associated their lace-making with the poverty of their homeland, but some wrote patterns and developed it into a beautiful handcraft. These patterns reflected the new way of life of their readers – exquisite opera bags, Christening bonnets, and fashionable collars. The parents of Percie Ryan travelled over from Tipperary during the Great Famine and settled in Dover, New Hampshire. As a young girl in the early twentieth century, Percie made some stunning pieces. An ardent reader of the *Dover Irish Crochet Pattern Book*, she lived to be 111 years old, dying in 1997. Her niece, Mary Lacombe sent me these samples of her valued work, requesting that she be remembered for her work.[60]

Percie Ryan's Irish Crochet Lace

Etta Harte, Kilready, New-townbutler, described this photograph:

It includes, from right to left, Miss K. Doherty (standing and showing the thread). The apron with the tuck-up at the bottom probably held balls of thread. Seated, with a headdress, a neigh-bour, next to my mother (Mary Conlon), who is also seated on a low stool. She has let her long plait of hair hang down and is wearing buttoned boots. Seated behind her is her mother (Elizabeth Con-lon) formerly Winters

Lace-makers at Drumsloe Lane, Clones

and an aunt of Josie (McCaffrey) Connolly's mother. Seated on my mother's left is her sister, Bridget and on extreme left is a cousin. This photo was taken at my mother's old home at Drumsloe, Connons, Clones, in the early part of the last century. The picture shows lace-making by women in their own homes. It was taken specially and in order to send copies to the USA to promote lace-making as a home (cottage) industry and to aid the export market. Misses Mary and Katie Doherty, Cara Street, Clones (where the Cosy Bar is now located) were buyers of the lace.

Lace-makers gathering in Pringle Hall, Clones 1967

Back row: *Brigid Boylan, Mary Jane Flynn (Clones), Kate McElroy (Magheraveely), Ellen Crudden, Maggie Lavery, Cassie O'Neill (Aghadrumsee), Mary Ann Dunwoody, Mary Anne Courtney, Rose Mohan (Clones)*
Middle row: *Nan Baxter (Roslea), Mrs Victory (Clones), Philomena Fitzpatrick, Annie Mc Cabe (Clones), Mary McIlgunn (Aghadrumsee), Mary Anne Mulligan, Mary Anne Killen*
Front row: *Eileen Crudden (Magheraveely), Vera Reilly (Clones), Annie Beggan (Clones), Bridie Mulligan (Corrany)*

MY INTRODUCTION TO CLONES LACE

In 1988, I first came to the historic town of Clones from Armagh – famous both as an ecclesiastical city and as an ancient Celtic capital, full of warrior sagas. Having set up a heritage project in the town, as part of my job, the history of Clones appealed to me. Mamo MacDonald, who was introduced to me, recalled the story of Clones lace, the local traditional craft. Always having had an interest in culture – playing traditional Irish music on the concertina and studying my native language, history and literature at degree level – the story of the local lace attracted me.

We decided to try to revive Clones lace, which had died out as a cottage industry in the area. There were examples of lace, made in the nineteenth century; still white, crisp and well cared for by their proud owners. That such an intricate and fine lace had developed against a backdrop of famine, disease and death, giving hope in an otherwise desolate period, fascinated me. On a summer's afternoon, while researching the lace-makers that were left in the area, we travelled up through the hills of Fermanagh and walked into Eileen Crudden's kitchen, where she sat, crocheting a shamrock doily. As we entered the room, she put her crochet away into a jam jar in which she kept her thread while working. Noticing that the hook had an unusual wooden handle, this glimpse from the past made a lasting impression on me.

Elizabeth Monahan

In that summer of 1988, a full-time training programme was set up for ten young women to learn Clones lace. It was very difficult to get someone who was able to teach the craft. All were either in ill health, or were caring for an elderly relative. We were very lucky that Elizabeth Monahan was willing to help us; she came from a lace-making tradition and kindly agreed to teach fine thread crochet one day a week. Others taught various aspects of wool crochet and marketing. Our aim was to set up a lace co-operative. Eileen McAleer, a member of that class remained with the Guild, which we set up in the summer of 1988. Elizabeth Monahan, though in bad health, continued to play her part and Raeleen Reavy, the youngest of the original ten, renewed her interest twelve years later, making a top in Clones lace and has now become one of our out-workers!

Raeleen Reavy

Nan Caulfield first introduced herself to us following the establishment of this original full-time course. The following spring, while the programme was still in progress, a night class was organised, taught by Nan. She demonstrated the Clones knot, as Mary Beggan of Roslea had shown her. Mary, whom I often visited, did the shamrock Clones knot as an edging around her prize-winning table centres. She died shortly after I had taken an interest in the lace and if she had not passed on her method of doing the Clones knot at that stage, it would probably have been lost. Nan also taught me how to crochet rose and shamrock squares, or trellis work. In the twentieth century, this 'fine work' had replaced the older 'heavy work', as the secrets and art of making and joining motifs had died out locally.

This more challenging floral work intrigued me, where the motifs, worked in very fine thread, using a thicker packing cord to shape the flowers, were joined by the Clones knot, or picot filling stitch. The packing cord gave the flowers their 'heavy' or 'coarse' appearance. Elizabeth Monahan and other local crocheters recalled, from their recollections, what flowers went together. Elizabeth used brown

Mary Ann Doran's piece – St Patrick's day 1912

Piece in progress and hook – courtesy of Jacqui Heurst

paper cut in shape as the template. Mamo gave me a small centre piece made by twelve-year-old Mary Ann Doran (later Dunwoody) which, according to family members, she joined behind a shed on St Patrick's day, 1912. I examined how the motifs were made and joined by the Clones knot.

Through this investigation, the secrets of Clones lace were revealed to me. Eithne D'Arcy, another local woman, played a key part in preserving the craft, by publishing a book on Irish crochet lace in 1984. Although this book undoubtedly helped me to work out how the motifs were crocheted, the recollections of Elizabeth, Nan and Mary were of greater benefit to me and within months of learning the craft, I was teaching the motifs and Clones knot.

Through the 1990s, we set up our business in the same way as it was done in the old days; trellis work – the squares, or 'pieces' as they are known locally – was worked in groups. One person made the centre rose or shamrock, another crocheted the square around it and a third joined it. A fourth might edge it. Sometimes the worker who dealt with the buyer bought rose squares or shamrock pieces off her neighbours and joined them herself. Today, one group of women, including the Cruddens and Tessie Leonard, all from Fermanagh, do the 'fine' trellis work – the rose and shamrock table centres and collars – as well as making insets and edging for linen hankies and tableware. These women have always crocheted and are carrying on a tradition handed down through their families, which they have perfected over a long period. The Cruddens have their own network of workers, mostly within their family circle, who help to complete linen and lace tableware, hankies edged with crochet or 'rose and shamrock' table centres. A group of women in Roslea, just five miles away, in county Fermanagh, were very successful in reviving the tradition of crochet lace-making there too and have had a weekly crochet class since 1993.

The older corded or guipure work, with its motifs and filling stitches, was also traditionally done by a number of people who contributed their own particular flower, while a final person designed the piece, filled between the motifs and edged the final piece. This was the only way that large orders could be completed in a short time, as it would take so long for one person to crochet a garment. In some cases, the worker would only know the section of work with which they were familiar. When we set up Clones Lace Guild, we followed this traditional method; four or five people make their own particular motifs, which I purchase from them by the dozen and then add a few motifs that are needed

to make a pattern, joining them with the Clones knot. This filling stitch is more open and it allows the motifs to stand out in the piece. The Bishop's Alb, which is one of showpieces of the exhibition in the Canal Stores, has been a great inspiration to us. It incorporates several types of lily and beautiful, though unusual flowers that were used to adorn altars. All the types of filling stitches, which would have featured in Clones lace in the past, join these. In modern Clones lace we never use the picot as a filling stitch, as it tends to 'crowd' the motifs. We use it as a trimming stitch.

Part of the vestments made for Dr McKenna, Bishop of Clogher in the early years of the twentieth century. This was made by a group of women in Monaghan and incorporates four distinct panels:
The host and chalice, with shamrock picot joining stitch.
Instruments of the Passion, with Clones knot filling stitch.
Initials 'SJ', with picot filling stitch.
Sacred Heart with rich 'buttony' joining stitch.
From private collection of Mamo MacDonald – on view in the Ulster Canal Stores, Clones

This is a very good example of Church lace, which was influenced by Venetian point lace and includes flowers that might have adorned an altar! This vestment was expertly adapted as a showpiece by Ellen and Annie Crudden, Magheraveely, county Fermanagh in the 1970s.

THE CASSANDRA HAND SUMMER SCHOOL
OF CLONES LACE

Since 1990, a lace-making summer school is held in Clones during the last week of June each year. The summer school is intimate and relaxing. Besides twenty-five hours of classes over five days, we like to recreate the social tradition of Clones lace-making; Two evening events are held during the week. We vary these events from year to year. The Cruddens always ensure that the group have a very enjoyable evening in Fermanagh, demonstrating how linen is hand-edged and 'done up' (while we enjoy their mouth-watering homemade baking). Ellen Todd, their cousin, whose mother Annie Ward was one of the Crudden sisters, has also entertained us with her crochet class in the Knocks, county Fermanagh. As part of the summer school, we often have a story-telling night when local lace-makers, such as Nan Caulfield and Elizabeth Monahan, gather in the Canal Stores to recollect stories about the old days, to the fascination of the visitors. The Sheelin Irish lace museum and shop, which is managed by Rosemary Cathcart, in Bellanaleck, county Fermanagh, has also become a favourite destination for the group, spending time examining the delicate antique lace, learning about other Irish laces and buying some of her latest acquisitions. We then relax in the restaurant next door over tea and homemade luscious desserts.

Cassandra Hand Summer School, July 1997

Giving a class in Seattle, 1999

For many years, Eithne D'Arcy officially opened the summer school in Mamo's Teashop. Indeed Mamo was deeply involved in it for years, leading the Cassandra Hand Trail around the landmarks associated with the foundress of the lace-making tradition. Her colourful stories of Lady Aberdeen or 'Blousy Bell' as she was fondly known and other characters associated with the lace-making tradition in the area, as we travelled around on this trail, made this tour a special event. In 1995, at the opening of a joint summer school of Clones and Carrickmacross laces, Mamo declared Monaghan as 'the Lace County of Ireland'! [61]

The Sarah Martin Lecture was also a feature of the summer school for years, with well-known personalities speaking at it. These included Linda Ballard of the Textiles Department at the Ulster Folk and Transport Museum, Cultra, Belfast; Thelma Goldring, who was awarded the Churchill Fellowship in 1983 for her work on Clones lace; Mairéad Dunleavy, Curator for Textiles at the National Museum of Ireland in Dublin; Sybil Connolly, an international couturier designer, famous in the 1960s for her Irish designs, especially for her pleated linen original evening dresses, which Jackie Onassis Kennedy made famous. Veronica Stuart – International Gold Medalist in lace-making – spoke at the writers' retreat in Annaghmakerrig as part of the 1995 'Celebrating Lace' joint summer school with Carrickmacross Lace Gallery. Veronica also gave a talk on Irish laces which she teaches, at our 2001 Summer School.

A young lace student, Clodagh McCarthy from county Kildare, presenting Sybil Connolly with flowers at the Cassandra Hand Summer School of Clones Lace – July 1993

I examine the work of Carol Ann McKenna in June 2000

40

Between 1990–2000, Eileen McAleer and I taught at these classes, with Elizabeth Monahan stepping in to relieve us. But as time goes on and circumstances change, we are changing the format of the school and bringing in new people to pass on the secrets of the craft. While the same people return each year, we always have a few new students. Jean Ness from California, who first came to the summer school in 1995, having read about it in *Victoria* magazine, has been returning to Clones each year. Many of the students stay with the hospitable Anne O'Harte, who gives us the use of her living room for weekend classes during the winter season! Most of the students have a large project that they concentrate on while in Clones, working on other crochet or craft projects at home.

Lillie Brady set up crochet classes in her local Active Age guild, having come to the Clones lace classes. Rosarii Flynn from Leitrim, started off in 1990 wanting to make a Christening robe for her niece. Over the years, the reason for the motifs changed into a Communion dress for the same child. They are now for her own Clones lace blouse. I joke that by the time she has the garment completed, it will be the shroud in which she will be 'laid out'. Although this is her main project, she has made v-neck collars and centre pieces in the inter-vening years. The summer school in-cludes all ages of lace-makers from 9–90! Students often bring along work that they have done using other techniques.

Lillie Brady and Rosarii Flynn. Lillie is working on a beautiful lampshade[62]

Josie McCusker from Emyvale has done exquisite full-length Carrickmacross wedding veils. In 2001, a group of four lace-makers from Cork brought along projects that they were working on in other Irish lace disciplines.

Mamo MacDonald and the Chinese ambassador in 1991.

WEEKEND COURSES

Ann Maher, who lives in Dublin, recently discovered our winter weekend classes and was overwhelmed to discover that 'such a fine and intricate craft' still existed. Lily Mooney travels from Dublin too. Her mother was Mary McGurk of Annaghkilly, Clones and 'a great crocheter'. Florence Creighton, one of our lace-making students, is a very warm and colourful character. Having learned to make a rose square in one of our classes in 1991, she left for a cookery competition in England, travelling to the competition in a van and entertaining the driver with her stories, while crocheting all the way. At the following week's class, most of the other students had finished one or two squares, whereas Florence returned with twenty perfect pieces, as well as first prize in the cookery competition and entertaining stories about her eventful week! I also travel to other areas to teach Clones lace and I often teach groups of children, including my own daughters and their friends. I don't make it as serious for them as it must have been for children in the past, when children completed several roses and shamrocks (heads) before school, or stayed away from school to complete large orders.

Children's class 2000. Clockwise: Máiréad Treanor, Máire, Olivia Curran, Clara Crudden, Eileen Crudden, Áine Treanor, Tara McKenna

Between 1995 and 1997, we organised a series of weekend classes in Clones with two teachers – Mary Wilson and Oonagh Mc Cullough – travelling from Banbridge, county Down, to teach the old crafts of sprigging and drawn thread work. Both classes were very popular, with students travelling from various parts of Ireland to attend. Dolores McGuigan, who embroiders personal messages onto our linen tableware, has become expert at sprigging tray cloths, onto which Tessie Leonard then crochets an edge. We also organise courses for groups, on request.

Artists in other mediums sign their work and usually become more famous when they die. In lace-making, as in other craftwork, the craftswoman's name is lost, except in folklore. Sarah McCabe from Cootehill unusually put a special shamrock into all her work, so as to identify it.[63] But there were very few women in the area with this foresight. Yet, today, as always, the story of Clones lace is, to a large extent, the story of the people who made it. Most of the motifs in this book are, therefore, named after the lace-makers of this locality as a tribute to their work. While this publication is aimed at the beginner, those who want more challenging patterns, should refer to the page 111 – 'Some Irish Crochet Publications'.

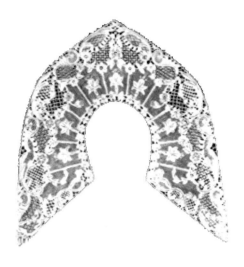

Youghal Needlepoint Lace: This is a true needle lace, all worked with sewing needle 'in the air'. It is based on Venetian point lace and Point de France, and was introduced as famine relief scheme in 1846. 200 gauge thread, or finer was used in nineteenth century. It is now made in DMC 30 or 50

Kenmare Lace: A flat needle lace and based on Venetian point lace, but the pattern relies more on motifs or flowers, with varied and more open filling stitches

Innishmacsaint Lace: This beautiful raised needlelace was made in the west Fermanagh area of Innishmacsaint and Derrygonnelly in the nineteenth century. It was first taught by the McClean sisters, who also introduced Tynan lace, which died out in the 1860s

Carrickmacross lace: This is the other great lace of county Monaghan. Based on Italian lace, a sewing needle is used to work the stitches. There are two types – Guipure and Applique. It is worked on ground net with organdie or muslin appliqued and fine cord couched around it to form pattern, then finished with fine needlepoint filling stitches and cut work. It is finally edged with tiny picots. In the recent past, it has been developed to include three-dimensional work.

Limerick laces: Both types are worked on net ground: Tambour and needlerun lace. In Tambour lace, a tambour hook, like a crochet hook, is used. Limerick Needlerun lace uses a small hoop too. It has a lighter appearance and a sewing needle is used.

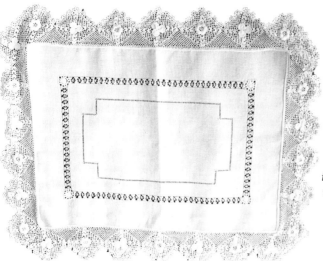

Drawnthread work: Threads are pulled in patterns. This is a very old craft and specimens are found throughout Europe. It was often worked on tableware with 'sprigging' embroidery in this area.

44

Irish crochet wedding dress: From the collection of Mrs McQuitty, Belfast, it is now part of Sheelin Museum collection in Bellinaleck, county Fermanagh. It incorporates examples of both Cork crochet lace where large flowers were joined by thick bars and Clones lace, with smaller flowers being joined by the Clones knot.

TYRONE

USNASKEA

FERMANAGH

ROSLEA

AGHADRUMSEE

SCOTSTOWN

MONAGHAN

NEWTOWN
BUTLER

CLONES

SMITHBOROUGH

KILLEEVAN

ONEWBLISS

SCOTSHOUSE

DRUM

MONAGHAN

BELTURBET

COOTEHILL

REDHILLS

CAVAN

ARMAGH

DERRY

BELFAST

MONAGHAN

CLONES

IRELAND

DUBLIN

GALWAY

CORK

46

VIEWS OF CLONES

Sunday afternoon in the Diamond, Clones

*Old cross and Church of Ireland, the
Diamond, Clones*

St Tiarnach's sarcophagus in the old round tower graveyard

The round tower

The 'wee abbey' graveyard in McCurtin Street

*McCurtin Street, where the lace makers sat outside their doors,
crocheting*

Cáit Treanor in Christening robe

*Charlene Browne in
wedding dress*

Máiréad, Máire and Áine Treanor

Tessie Leonard

Doirean Christening robe

Christening wear made by Clones Lace Guild, 1990–1999

This photograph shows family Christening bonnet on a fuschia bush from my own garden. I made the fuschia motif from this bush, which I included in the bonnet. This photo was made into a postcard in 1993, which was sold to visitors to Clones

Áine Treanor in family Clones lace Communion head dress, May 1999

Cáit Treanor in a Clones lace and Irish linen Communion dress, May 2000

Shannon Donnelly wearing jeans, jewellery and hairpieces made and designed by her mother Paula Donnelly, Ballymaguigan, county Derry, after taking Clones lace/ Irish crochet classes over four weeks, using the basic patterns in this publication and her imagination!

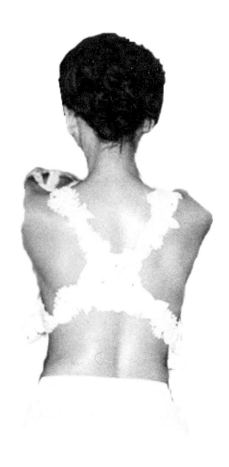

Clones lace takes to the International stage. Top made by Clones lace-makers for Irish designer, Lainey Keogh, modelled in Paris, 1994

Top made and designed by Máire Treanor for Tracy McGuigan, 2000

Clones lace and Irish crochet tableware by Máire Treanor and Tessie Leonard

Some ideas for your motifs. Oval table centre by Eileen Crudden

Above: Some Irish crochet table centres

Below: Some Clones lace collars and accessories

HOW TO MAKE CLONES LACE

BEGINNERS

People often say that they would love to learn Clones lace, but it looks so difficult! It only looks difficult. Once you learn the basic crochet stitches, you can do it! The most challenging part is the Clones knot, which is why everybody wants to learn it. Practice makes perfect!

If you are a beginner, you can learn Clones lace, by practising the various stitches first. When I am teaching a beginner, whether a child or an adult, I simply ask them to become practiced at the chain stitch, to get the feel of the thread and hook. Make it as long as you like. Make a necklace out of it, or as long as yourself! It is good practice to become accustomed to the hook and fine thread. When you are comfortable with this simple stitch, you are then ready to start on a small rose. You will learn most of the stitches in this simple flower. Don't be too concerned about doing all the various stages at the beginning. If a flower looks too difficult, miss it. You can always go back to it later on. Now try a wild rose, which finishes off with the packing cord. Use No. 20 mercerised thread and No. 1.25 hook. Always use No. 20 mercerised thread for PC, whether you are using No. 20 to crochet with, or a finer thread.

When you have gone through all the patterns and projects in this book, you will be proud that you can make Clones lace. If you are still curious, there are lots of older pattern books that you can investigate through your local library!

Experienced crochet workers won't follow these patterns step by step, but will make changes that work for them. If you are a beginner and you find that they aren't working out for you, just do it whatever way feels and looks right for you to get the same effect as the finished photo.

LEFT HANDERS

As a left-handed writer myself, I am probably more aware than most of the problems and prejudices which left-handers have to overcome.[64] Thankfully, being a left-hander is an advantage to me and although I taught myself to crochet with my right hand, I can go left or right without having to turn my work. I first saw a left-handed crochet worker Methona McNally doing this and followed her example.[65] Some left-handers might simply need to think of the instructions in a mirror fashion. Remember, being left-handed is not an impediment to crocheting!

This centre was made by Liza Gunn and the Cruddens of Magheraveely in the 1960s.[66]

THREAD AND HOOK GUIDE

THREAD	IRISH HOOKS (STEEL)	US HOOK SIZES
No. 10 (Mercerised)	1.50	#10
No. 20 (Mercerised)	1.25, 1.00	#12
No. 40 (Mercerised)	.75	#13
No. 60 (Mercerised)	.60	#14
No. 80 (Mercerised)	.50	#15
No. 100 (Mercerised)	.50, .40	#16
No. 40 (Cotton)	.50	#15
No. 50 (Cotton)	.50, .40	#16

USA	IRISH
CH = Chain	CH = Chain
DC = Double crochet	TR = Treble
SC = Single crochet	DC = Double crochet
TR = Treble	DTR = Double treble
HDC = Half double crochet	HTR = Half treble

ABBREVIATIONS:
CH = Chain; S kn = Slip knot; SS = Slip Stitch; TR = Treble; DTR = Double Treble;
DC = Double Crochet; ST = Stitch; PC = Packing Cord; CK = Clones Knot; P = Picot.

Irl = Chain
US = Chain

Irl – Double crochet [dc]
US = Single crochet [sc]

Irl = Treble [tr]
US = Double crochet [dc]

Irl = Half treble
US – Half double crochet [hdc]

Irl = Slip stitch [ss]
US = Slip stitch [ss]

Irl = picot
US = picot

51

THE STITCHES

To start crocheting:

Wrap thread around left hand. You should attempt to have the thread in the right position, but at the 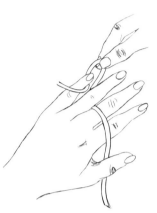 beginning, just hold it whichever way is easiest for you. You can go back later on, and learn how to do it the right way. At the beginning, don't try to learn too many things at the one time, or you will get burdened, and give up! Remember – we all had to learn. It is important though to learn this early on, as it will ensure you have a good tension. Another tip to ensure good tension is always to pull the thread gently, when you make a stitch.

To maintain a tension in your thread:

Hold tail of thread between thumb and index finger; then over the first and second fingers.

Continue it under the third and fourth fingers.

Wrap thread around small last finger.

Hold second finger straight up, with a space of 1" between first and second fingers, as you will be using this space for the hook.

Hold the hook in your right hand, as if you were holding a pencil.

SLIP KNOT: (S KN)

With thread in position around left hand, hold it 1" from end, between thumb and index finger.

Bring hook left to right under thread.

Turn hook backwards towards tail.

Hook under thread again and pull another loop through it.

Gently tighten and slide the loop up the hook.

CHAIN STITCH: (CH)

Thread over hook, anti-clockwise.

Pull through stitch on hook already, to form a new loop. (1 CH made.)

Thread over anti-clockwise.

Pull through stitch on hook (2 CHs).

Pull firm, but not too tight …

Continue for specified number of stitches.

It is a good idea to practice making a long chain, so that you become familiar with it.

SLIP STITCH: (SS)

Hook into work.

Thread over hook.

Pull through both the work and loop on
hook in one movement, so that just one
stitch remains.

You can pull hook through 2 stitches, then
thread over hook, and pull through to
make 1 stitch.

Gently pull thread tight each time.

The slip stitch can be used to join and bring thread from one place to another, being the shortest
crochet stitch.

DOUBLE CROCHET: (DC – SC IN US)

Hook into work.

Catch thread with hook.

Pull back out through work.

Thread over hook.

Pull thread through 2 stitches. (1 stitch left on hook.)

(Always hold hook downwards, and bring thread in anti-clockwise way.)

HALF TREBLE: (HTR)

Thread over hook anti-clockwise.

Hook into work.

Thread over hook.

Hook out of work again.

Thread over hook.

Pull hook through all 3 stitches on hook, so that one stitch remains.

TREBLE: (TR – DC IN US)

Thread over hook.

Hook into work.

Thread over hook.

Hook out of work again.

Thread over hook, anti-clockwise.

Pull through 2 stitches on hook.

Thread over hook again.

Pull through two remaining stitches.

(1 stitch left on hook.)

DOUBLE TREBLE: (DTR)

Thread over hook twice.

Hook into work.

Thread over hook.

Hook out of work again.

Thread over hook anti-clockwise.

Pull through 2 stitches on hook.

Thread over hook.

Pull through 2 stitches.

Thread over hook again and pull through 2 remaining stitches.

(1 stitch left on hook.)

PICOT

CH 4.

SS into first CH.

Pull thread gently.

CH according to pattern.

THE CLONES KNOT (CK)

There are several ways to do the Clones knot:

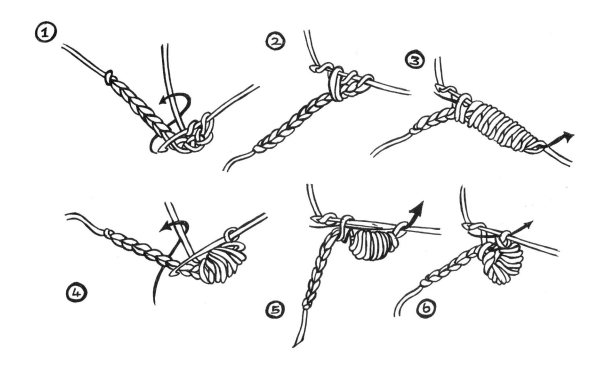

Use a mercerised coarse thread and hook for practice, e.g., 1.25 hook and 20 mercerised thread. This knot is formed on a length of chain.

Make 8 CH.

Catch the eighth stitch firmly between the forefinger and the needle.

Hold it there while hooking the thread alternatively over and under the CHs until there are about 20 loops on the hook.

You will see that the chain is covered with the loops.

Insert the hook through the first CH.

Loop the thread over the hook, and draw it through all the loops on the hook.

The eighth stitch must be held until this is done, otherwise the stitch is spoiled.

Draw up the knot closely by gently pulling the thread over the fingers.

Put the hook under the stem of the knot and form a tight SS.

The knot is then secured in place by a DC into the motif, or in practice, make a further 8 CH.

MY CLONES KNOT

I learned this Clones knot from Mary Beggan, just before she died. It is very easy to follow, when shown it, but this is the first time it has been put on paper!

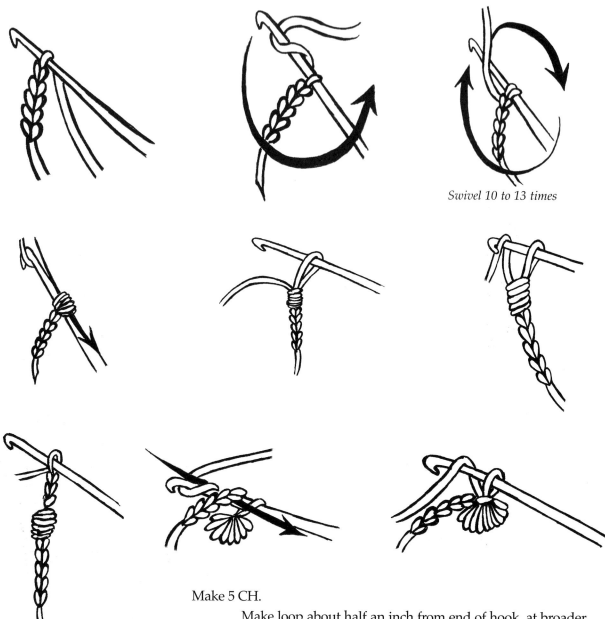

Swivel 10 to 13 times

Make 5 CH.

Make loop about half an inch from end of hook, at broader part. This is very important, as it will make it easier to pull the thread through later on.

Swivel the hook left, backwards, then right, catching thread under the hook left and right, 10 to 13 times, depending on thickness of thread.

Bring the hook under the thread, and pull it easily through the knot made.

Make SS over the top of the knot.

Make 2 CH and SS left of the knot. Gently pull thread tight each time.

Make 5 CH … Connect CH to motif with slip stitch, or on second and consecutive rows in trellis fashion.

SS on right side of knot of previous row and then on left side of knot, pulling thread tight each time. Continue and fill in between motifs.

When you are practising the Clones knot, use a thick thread (20 mercerised cotton thread and 1.25 hook) and make a long chain, as you practiced the chain stitch at the beginning. When you are comfortable with it, cut the thread about an inch from the hook, pull the thread right through, make 1 CH and pull the thread tight. When you have learned how to do the wild rose, try the project on page 100 (the wild rose brooch).

Cynthia Stewart, a young designer who marketed Clones lace in the US under an Ireland Fund programme 1993. Some antique Clones lace samples are on the panel

TIPS!

TO START OFF:

The centre of a motif is usually begun on a ring. Make a slip knot (see guide for slip knot on page 52). The older lace-makers started off without a slip knot. This takes practice, though. They also made a knot at the beginning of their work to stop it pulling through. They would pull through the beginning thread through their work, when they were finished.

FINISH OFF:

Make SS. Make 2 CHs. Cut half an inch from CHs. Pull thread through loop and pull tightly. Cut thread closer. This is the way the people finished off their work in the past in this area. It is a more secure way to finish off.

WORKING DOWN SIDE OF MOTIF:

When you come to the top end of a petal, rather than finish off and cut thread, continue down to centre of motif with 2 CHs and SS into each loop, to bottom of petal and centre. Be ready to start on next petal, eg., wild rose, clematis, or three-ringed shamrock. There is a risk of the thread unravelling if you cut thread at top of petal.

TENSION:

Always pull thread gently, when you finish a stitch, to keep the tension firm. But don't pull it too tightly, or you will not be able to pull the hook through the next stitch. This is the main difference between wool and thread crochet!

PLACING THE MOTIFS ON THE TEMPLATE:

To get the motifs into the same position on both sides, centre-fold the material or paper template following the same line with fingers, before pinning them on. Crochet one row of the joining stitch around each motif. Then tack them on when you are happy that they are in the same position on both sides.

TO MAKE STEM:

Join PC to thread, in centre of bunch of grapes. Make 35 DC over PC. Connect to vine leaf, in centre point, with SS. Stretch out DCs along PC. Turn and make DCs around PC into back of DCs just made. Pull PC gently. Finish off.

DECREASE:

When decreasing loops in motif, make 2 CHs and SS into first and last loops of previous row. 4 CH loop as usual.

INCREASE:

When increasing 1 loop in motif, make 2 loops into first and last loops of previous row.

WORKING ON TURN:

Always work 1 CH on the turn, to make it easier to turn. Experienced crochet workers will do this automatically.

TO MAKE A PADDED CIRCLE IN CENTRE OF FLOWER:

First way: Make specified number of CHs, followed by DCs on PC. SS last ST to first ST, pulling thread tight. Then pull PC tight into circle.

Second way: Wrap thread around a knitting needle 13 times, then make 18 DCs around loop.

Third way: Make 15 CH, catch last CH to first CH, make 18 DC around loop. SS last DC to first DC.

Twenty-one Motifs

SMALL ROSE

The small rose is the first motif that most crochet workers learn. It is used as a centre for other motifs and for Irish crochet squares. You will use all the stitches – the slip stitch, the chain stitch, the double crochet and the treble. These stitches are also used in wool crochet. This is the most common flower in Irish crochet.

Practice with No. 20 mercerised thread and No. 1.25 hook

Always use No. 10 or 20 mercerised thread for PC.

Make S kn then 7 CH. Join last to first stitch with SS, to make circle.

Make 5 CH. 1 TR into the circle (then 3CH, 1TR into circle). Repeat 3 times. (5 loops). 3 CH. SS to first loop made to complete circle

(1DC, 3TR, 1DC, SS) into first loop of previous row, to make first petal. Repeat 5 times – first row of 6 petals.

5 CH. Connect with SS, between bars that you made in row 2. Repeat 5 times.

(1 DC, 5TR, 1DC, SS) into each loop just made, to make second row of petals.

Finish off here, or you can continue to make third row of petals.

(7 CH. Connect with SS) between each of petals of fourth row.

(1DC 7 TR 1DC SS) into each loop of sixth row, to make third row of petals.

Finish off.

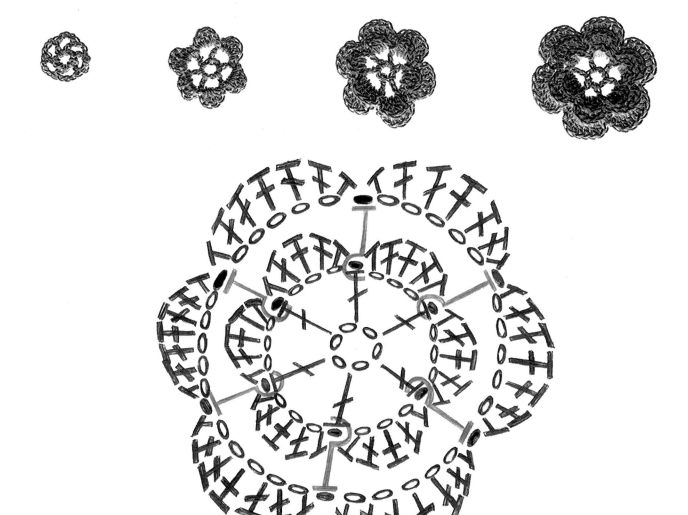

60

Mary Beggan's Small Rose

Mary Beggan from Roslea, took a class in Glaslough, county Monaghan, in the 1970s, showing her students how to do the rose this way. One of them, Alice Connolly now occasionally comes to my workshops. I think this centre is nice in fine squares.

Start with 15 CH. Catch the last stitch to the first stitch with SS to make a circle.

Make 18 DC around the circle.

Make 5 CH and TR into third DC. Continue with 3 CHs and TRs, evenly spaced out. To make sixth loop, 3 CH, and SS into first loop. You will now have 6 loops.

For petals (1DC, 3 TR, 1DC, SS) into first loop, repeat 5 more times.

Make 5 CH, catch with SS into TRs in row 3, working from back to front. Continue 5 more times. This is the basis of the next row of petals.

Make (1 DC, 5 TR, 1 DC, SS) into first loop.
Repeat 5 more times. Finish off.

The Wild Rose

This is one of the most common motifs in this area. It is also one of the easiest to learn, incorporating all the aspects of Clones lace – the rose, the various stitches and finishing with the packing cord. Tessie McMahon crocheted this motif for the guild for ten years, but has retired from crocheting. Thankfully, Raeleen Reavy, a younger crochet worker is happy to take on the work, continuing the tradition!

Practice with No. 20 mercerised thread and No. 1.25 hook
Always use No. 20 mercerised thread for PC.

Rose Centre:
This rose centre is like the small rose, except that there are 5 petals, rather than 6 and two rows of petals.

Make S Kn and 6 CH. Join last stitch to first stitch in a circle.

Make 5 CH, 1TR into circle. * 3 CH, 1 TR. * Repeat * to * twice more. 3 CH. Join to first loop in circle.

To make petals: (1 DC, 3TR, 1 DC, SS) into first space. Repeat 4 times, to complete first row of petals.

To make basis for second row (make 5 CH and SS) into each bar that you made in stage 3.

Make (1 DC, 5 TR, 1 DC, SS) into first space. Repeat 4 times, to make second row of petals.

Petals for Wild Rose:

7 CH. Connect with SS between each of petals of previous row.

Now, working each petal separately, * make 10 DC into first loop of first row.

Turn, and make loop (4 CH, SS) into every second DC just made. (5 loops.)

Turn, and continue making 4 CH and SS into each loop of previous row for 5 more rows, ending on front (left) side.

Work down side of petal to base with 2 CH and SS into each loop. One petal is now complete. SS into centre. *

SS into next loop, and continue as for first petal * to * for each of next 4 petals.

Always complete flower with a row of doubled PC around petals. Take thick cord (10 or 20 mercerised). Measure from hand to elbow, double and cut. Make SS through fold, then over PC:

Working over PC, crochet around flower with DCs up side of petal – roughly 2 DCs to each loop.

Keeping PC with you, on topside, (1DC, 5 TR, 1DC) into first loop.

(1DC, 3TR, 1DC) into 3 middle loops.

(1DC, 5TR, 1DC) into last loop. – 5 loops along top.

Work down side with DCs – 2 DCs to each loop.

SS into bottom centre.

When you are finished, cut PC close to flower and finish off thread in usual way.

(If you run out of PC, just cut more, double as before, join in and continue.)

THE CLEMATIS

The inspiration for the Clematis came from my garden. I designed this flower in 1992, being quite fond of my own lilac clematis. I am sure, though, that a similar flower made in the past, died out. My garden clematis has long since withered. I am too busy making lace for orders to have time for gardening!

Practice with No. 20 mercerised thread, and No. 1.25 hook.

Always use No. 10 or 20 mercerised thread for PC.

Make 15 DC around doubled PC. SS last ST to first ST and pull PC into a circle. Drop PC.

To give stamen effect around the flower, * crochet 5 CH, SS to first DC, giving a picot effect. SS into second DC on circle. * 5 CH again. SS into same DC. Repeat * to* around circle. (15 Ps).

To start petals, crochet 4 CH, SS to fourth DC on base circle that you made in stage 1. Repeat 4 times around circle. These loops should be spread evenly around circle, and form a basis for the petals.

For first petal, crochet 6 DC into first loop.

Turn. Crochet 4 CH, SS into every second DC. (3 loops.)

In next row, increase to 5 loops by making 2 loops into first and last loop of previous row. Continue for 4 more rows, ending on front left row.

Start decreasing, by making 2 CH into first loop. Then continue with 4 CH loops to end of row.

Turn, and make 2 CH, SS to first loop, as before. Continue decreasing in this way until 1 loop remains (make 5 CH in the final loop) ending on front left row. Work down to base of petal (2 CH, SS into petal, 2 CH … and SS to base circle.)

Repeat for 4 more petals, finishing off at PC, which you should have left since first row.

Make DCs around PC around edge of petals to give firmness to flower – 2 DC to each loop.

In top middle loop of petal, make 3 DC, P, 3 DC around PC. (Pull PC firm at top of petal.) Continue to end of petal and pull PC firm, pulling petal into shape.

Continue for all petals to end. If you run out of PC, just cut more, and join in as before.

Cut PC and finish off.

NAN CAULFIELD

After a long hunt for someone to teach us Clones lace-making, Nan Caulfield, or the 'Beauty Quigley', as she was known in her native Roslea in her young days, came in to see me in the maternity ward of Monaghan hospital in 1989. As a result of her visit, she later took a workshop in Clones. I was amongst her pupils. She was my first teacher of Irish crochet squares and demonstrated the Clones knot and the Shamrock Clones knot as she had seen Mary Beggan of Roslea do them. Mary did the Shamrock Clones knot as an edging to table centres in fine trellis work. Nan is a colourful personality and a regular participant in our *Cassandra Hand Summer School*, entertaining us with her numerous stories of the lace-making tradition in the Clones-Roslea area at the lace storytelling night. In the past, she entered competitions at country fairs and often brought along a prize-winning entry for us to see. In 1993 she entered the Tydavnet Summer Fair with a table centre made out of cord tops of meal bags, which the neighbouring farmers left hanging over the top of their gates for her to

collect. She washed the cord and made a 'pineapple centre' of 18″ diameter, which won her first prize! When Nan was young, children practiced their crochet stitches with the cord from the tops of meal bags. Her aunt, Elizabeth Quigley, taught an Irish crochet school in Blacksod Bay, county Mayo.

THE SHAMROCK

The shamrock is sometimes called the cloverleaf. This pattern uses the packing cord all the time.

*Make a SS through the join of the PC (see guide). Make (2 DC, 16 TR, 2 DC, SS) all over PC.

To join leaf, make SS into first DC, and pull cord into circular shape, holding leaf with thumb and index finger.

Continue in an anti-clockwise direction. Keeping the PC with you, 1 DC into each stitch of last row, making 2 DC into every third TR (approx. 27 DC when this row is finished).

Make SS into first DC and pull cord into shape * Make sure that leaf is flat. If it is curled up, you have pulled it too tight!

Repeat * to * twice more to complete shamrock.

As an embellishment to the shamrock and to cover the centre of the shamrock, you can place a 'buttony' in middle of shamrock and attach to leaves, securing shamrock at same time – make SS on 'buttony' and on each side of leaf. 5 CH worked at back of leaf. Repeat for second and third leaves.

Finish off.

You can also put a Clones knot in the centre of the shamrock, rather than the buttony, when you learn how to do it.

SPRAYS

If you are a beginner, skip the following sprays. Come back to them when you are a bit more experienced!

MY SHAMROCK SPRAY

You can make a shamrock for the front of a v-neck collar, like I always do. Don't finish off when you have made the shamrock. (See photo of collar page 106.)

Make shamrock. Then make 8 DC over the PC, 2 CH to mark division.

10 DC again. 2 CH again. Make another shamrock, 10 DC down into the backs of the last 10 DC.

8 DC, over PC, on their own, 2 CH, 12 DC, another shamrock.

Continue, working it out for yourself, and follow the picture.

Make 3 shamrocks up one side, then 3 on other side, working DCs into back of main stem.

Alternatively, you can make 7 shamrocks separately and join them in the spray. Mariam Savage does hers differently. This is why handwork is so interesting!

MARIAM'S SHAMROCK SPRAY

Make 4 shamrocks separately.

Join the PC with a SS to the first shamrock. Make 15 DC around the PC.

Join in another shamrock with a SS. Make 15 DC.

Join third and fourth shamrocks in same way on the spray.

Turn and work DCs into back of work, keeping PC with work. When you are finished, cut PC. Make
  2 CH and cut thread.

*When you are putting this spray onto a collar, or other work, tack on, using your imagination. Make opposite one
in same way.*

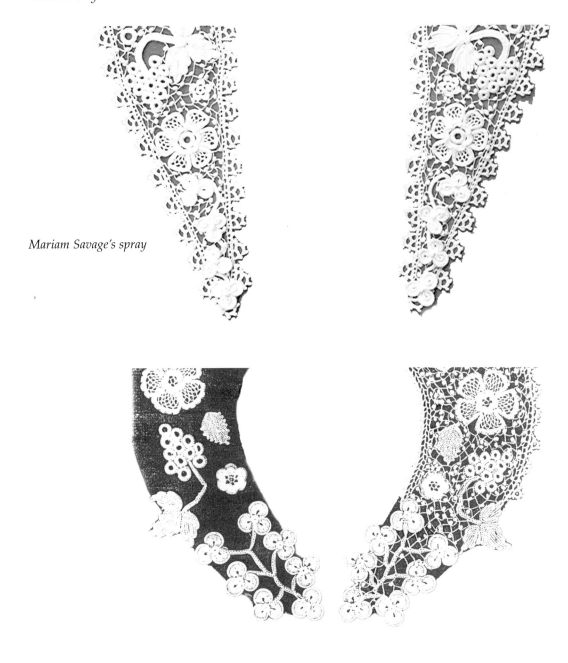

Mariam Savage's spray

My shamrock spray

Make 3 shamrocks and 1 harp.

To join motifs with spray, SS thread to first shamrock. 10 DC over PC.

2 CH alone. 10 DC over PC.

Join in second shamrock. Turn.

10 DC down backs of previous 10 DC, over PC.

Work 10 DC on PC alone. Join in third Shamrock.

Turn and work into backs of 10 DC, over PC.

10 DC on PC alone. Join in harp. Turn.

20 DCs in to backs of DCs – back to first shamrock.

Finish off.

SUSAN SHEILS

Susan Sheils was one of the finest lace-makers in the Clones area earlier in this century.[67] She was especially skilled at joining lace to linen, which was a craft in itself. I first heard of her in the summer of 1992, when I got a phone call from her daughter, Annie, asking me to call and collect some lace. I found my way to her home in Cullintra, near Cavan. Annie, in her eighties stood at the door of a country cottage, waiting for me. She brought me into an old-style kitchen and showed me a box of motifs, which her mother Susan had made many years ago. She offered to sell the threads, linen, and motifs, which I bought from her at a fair price.

Susan Sheils and her daughter Annie

Susan was born in 1892 in Edergole, in county Cavan, and started crocheting in 1904 at the age of 12. She went to school in Bunnoe, county Cavan. A lace teacher came to the school, giving them classes in lace-making. She was good at the lace and used to get a train from Redhills to Clones to sell it on market day. When she married she moved to Pottle West, which was in the same area.[68] She took a break from the crocheting, but started it again to support her growing family in 1944. Neighbouring women including Mrs Reilly and Mrs Flood, worked for her. They made the pieces, which she either joined or inserted into table cloths and vestments.

Miss Leonard of Roslea bought gloves and centres from Susan Sheils, who exchanged the crochet for groceries. This was a 'bartering system' that was very common with the lace workers. She also worked for Murnanes of Ballybay and she made Church vestments for Mrs Mullany of O'Neill Park in Clones (the former Elizabeth Quigley). Susan got 3s. 6d. for a yard of crochet edging.

In later years, she used to get a bus from Cavan to Clones and sold tableware to Mary Kilcoyne. When Mary died, Susan sold the lace to Olive Byrne, who remembers her as 'a very calm, gentle woman in a black coat and hat'.[69] On special occasions in Clones, Olive displays one of Susan's supper cloths in her window over a small round table. Susan died in 1979 at the age of 87.

The Harp

In 1999, when I was teaching Clones Lace-Irish Crochet at the CGOA Annual Conference in Seattle, on hearing that I played traditional Irish music on the concertina, Therese Honey disappeared and returned a few minutes later with her Brian Ború Harp to serenade us, while we crocheted. I wrote out the pattern of the harp for her.

Crochet 18 CH. Crochet 4 CH. SS into third CH from last stitch.

Continue, making 4 CH loops and SS to every second CH to end of row. (9 loops) Turn.

2 CH, SS into first loop of row. Continue with 4 CH loops to end of row. Turn.

Continue, decreasing by two loops on each row until only one loop remains. Make 5 CH for last top loop.

Bring in PC. To finish off edge of harp, crochet 2 DCs to every loop, working around PC.

Make 5 DC on each corner. Continue around 3 sides of harp.

Therese Honey takes a break from her Irish crochet class in Seattle to play the harp, 1999

Continue around harp with DCs and PC a second time. On first corner, make 10 DC around PC alone. SS into base DC. Pull PC. Make another 10 DC on PC alone and SS into same DC. Pull PC into circle. Make another 10 DC on PC alone. (3 circles.) Pull PC again and SS into same DC.

On second corner, make 10 DC on PC alone and SS to base DC.

On third corner, make 3 picots (5 CHs in each P) into same DC.

2 DCs to end of row. Finish off.

You might like to add strings to your harp.
Rejoin your thread between the first row of DC on the outside rim of the harp, at the shortest point. Make 4 or 5 CH. SS to lower point.
Crochet 6 or7 CH. Continue like this, increasing until you have made about 10 strings on the harp.
You might like to decorate the harp more. Go ahead. Use your own imagination!

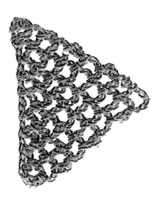

ANNETTA HUGHES' SMALL VINE LEAF

Annetta Hughes is from Ture, between Clones and Newbliss. She has been working for the Lace Guild since 1990. She is the person to whom we turn when we want something such as Christmas decorations done and she is very

good at Irish crochet centres, made in one piece. Her mother also made these Irish crochet centres. She also makes the small vine leaf or ivy leaf, as it is sometimes called, and the daisy.

At this stage you should be moving down to No. 40 thread and .75 hook.

Make leaves separately, joining them together, when you have finished each one.

All work is done around PC.

To make middle leaf:

16 CH. Bring in PC, with SS. Turn. Working over PC, make 16 DC into row of CHs just made. On last chain, crochet 3 DC.

Continue up other side of work and make 16 DC over PC into back of work. 3 DC into last DC.

Continue on upside with DCs, keeping PC with work all the time. Work to last 4 DCs. Turn with 1 CH.

Work into DCs of previous row. Make 3 DC into bottom middle DC and work up left side to last 4 DCs. 1 CH to turn.

Work down into backs of DCs. Continue like this until there are 3 layers on each side of leaf. Finish off on upside.

Cut PC before you finish off.

To make other leaves:

The second and third leaves can have 2 or 3 layers, depending on your preference. I prefer to have 2 layers.

For 2 layered leaves, start with 14 CH, and continue as you did for the first leaf, but finish after 2 layers on upside.

When you have finished second leaf, join it to the first leaf with SSs. Place 2 sides of leaves together, so that they meet at same point at bottom. Make SSs through tops of DCs down one side of each leaf. Continue to the bottom. Finish off.

Join third leaf to first centre leaf in same way. Finish off.

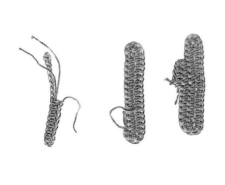

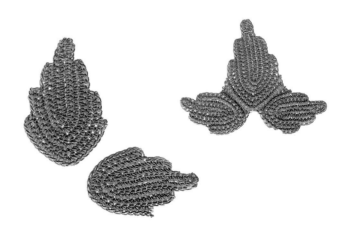

THE LARGE VINE LEAF

I designed this vine leaf, based on one that I got from Elizabeth Monahan, which was made by her Aunt Liza, making some small changes to it. The vine leaf is similar to the small vine leaf, except for the open effect up through the middle of the leaves. There are five sections in it, rather than three. I am very fond of the grape and vine, which have always been a central feature of my designs and they have become a hallmark of my work.

All the following work should be done over the PC:

First Leaf: Make 18 CH. Join in PC and work 18 DC up back of CHs.

Make 3 DC into last DC and make 18 DC down other side of previous row, bringing PC with you.

At end of row, make 5 DCs on PC alone. Miss 2 DCs at bottom and continue up other side of leaf, working to fourth DC from end of row. Pull PC gently.

Work down again and make 5 DCs on PC alone in centre. Pull PC gently. This gives an open effect down the centre of the leaf.

Repeat until you have 3 layers on each side of leaf. Finish off. This is your centre leaf.

Second and third leaves: Make 16 CH. Bring in PC and repeat as for first leaf.

Join second and third leaves to first leaf. Join in same way as with the small vine leaf.

Fourth and fifth leaves: Make 15 CH. Bring in PC and repeat as for other leaves, but this time, only make 2 layers on each side.

71

An Embellishment

Embellishments are additions to the flower, giving it a three-dimensional effect. They are usually made up either of buttonies or small flower centres. Tessie Leonard calls this centre the 'clock', which she made as a child for her mother's lilies. The buyer paid the lace-maker extra money for work with this additional centre on it.

With PC still on spool, double back 2". Make 15 DC around PC. SS last stitch to first stitch to make circle. Go around PC again, increasing to keep the circle flat. Then with single PC, make 10 DC on PC alone.

SS into base stitch. Pull PC into circle. Make 2 SS into backs of DCs that make up circle. Make 10 DC on PC alone. SS into base stitch. Pull PC. Repeat 8 more times (10 circles).

To attach embellishment to vine leaf, do not cut thread. SS the embellishment to vineleaf. Make 3 CHs on back of work. SS, joining embellishment to vineleaf. Repeat until embellishment is secured to vineleaf.

Elizabeth Monahan

Elizabeth Monahan was born into a lace-making family. Her Aunt Liza left Derrylin in county Fermanagh and went to Mayo, then Bruckless in county Donegal in the 1920s, where she became the owner of the lace industry there. Elizabeth's mother, sisters and all her neighbours worked for Liza.

Her sister, Kate went to Bruckless at an early age and spent her working life there, in the laundry of Liza's lace factory. Elizabeth recalls: 'I started learning my lace-making at the age of five years, watching my sister and a neighbour while they worked. I remember the first thing I made was what they called a 'buttony' – a number 10 thread was rolled around a suitably sized piece of round stick, and then double crochets were worked around it until it was completely covered in. It was a great achievement for a five year old, or so I thought.'

From this beginning, Elizabeth progressed to making flowers to be joined together to make adornments for all kinds of dress ware, blouses, tray cloths and gloves. As a married woman in Clones, she crocheted a blouse during her nine pregnancies, adding a section during each stay in the local nursing home. She taught fellow ICA members in Clones and we were very fortunate to have her teach part-time in a FÁS class that was organised on Clones lace in 1988. When I first became interested in Clones lace, Elizabeth gave me a lot of her aunt's old vine leaves which I incorporated into a wedding dress for the 1990 World Trade Fair in Ossaka. She also gave me some old maniloves thread, which is now part of the exhibition in the Canal Stores. She explained to me which motifs traditionally went together and provided guidelines on how the motifs were put together on a brown paper template. She is a regular participant in the storytelling night at the summer school each year and continues to pass her knowledge on to others.

THE MAPLE LEAF

The Maple leaf is made in a similar way to the vine leaf, except that you make 5 DC around PC on each turn. Cynthia Stewart and myself worked out how to make a maple leaf one night, when Cynthia was designing a piece for a Canadian dignitary, who had come to Monaghan as part of the Monaghan–Prince Edward Island celebrations in 1998. This maple leaf is actually closer to the old vine leaf that Liza Gunn did. As in Liza's vine leaf, I put a buttony rather than a 'clock' as the embellishment on it. You are free to do whichever you wish.

BUTTONY

'Buttony' is the local term used. Other books might refer to 'buttons'.

Wrap thread around 13 times.

With thumb and index finger, take circle off knitting needle and make first DC with crochet hook on circle.

Continue around with DCs (approx. 18) until circle is filled.

Catch last stitch to first stitch with SS. Crochet 1 CH stitch. Cut thread half an inch from end. Pull thread through loop. Finish off.

Make 12 'buttonies'. Don't cut twelfth one.

Join 'buttonies' together with SSs, in the shape that is shown below

When you have joined 12, join PC at top of grape and make spray to vine leaf.

THE BUNCH OF GRAPES

Elizabeth Monahan first taught me how to make the Bunch of Grapes.

You will need a No. 4mm (or No. 8 knitting needle, child's knitting needle, crochet hook). I used the top of a pen for the buttonies in this pattern. I have also wrapped the thread around my finger for bigger buttonies, to make the '0' in '2000'!

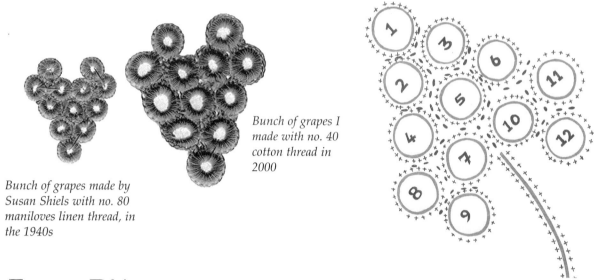

Bunch of grapes I made with no. 40 cotton thread in 2000

Bunch of grapes made by Susan Shiels with no. 80 maniloves linen thread, in the 1940s

EITHNE D'ARCY

Eithne D'Arcy who came from Clones, lived in nearby Roslea all her married life. Her family, the McGorrys, were lace buyers in the Diamond in Clones. A lot of her extensive collection would have

come from her family.

Unfortunately, when I was learning Clones lace, I was not able to visit her in Roslea easily, due to the inevitable delays in travel caused by road closures and military delays along the border. I didn't get to know her until she was in her eighties and in ill health. By this time she had stopped crocheting. She remarked on a piece that I found particularly attractive (the 'Shamrock Clones Knot' jabot that her daughter, Daphne, let me borrow to be photographed for this book, see page 75) that it had been made by an old woman who lived up in the hills of Fermanagh and was brown-black when finished, but after being laundered in the McGorry business, it became delicate and beautiful.

Eithne officially opened our *Cassandra Hand Summer School of Clones Lace* for several years and was guest of honour at functions that we organised. When she was younger, in the 1960s, she ran a business, getting blouses made-to-order by out-workers in Roslea in the 1960s. Other workers in the area, such as Maggie Murray of the Racecourse in Clones, who had worked for her family in Clones, made motifs for blouses, which she joined. Her daughter Daphne remembers that she had large brown paper templates spread out on the table with motifs tacked on them.[70] Elizabeth Monahan remembers her Aunt Liza staying with Eithne, passing on her experience and knowledge to her, in the 1960s. At her funeral in November 1999, I met a woman, whose mother, Mrs Slowey of Roslea, was one of these out-workers. She said that her mother made 8 or 9 flowers every night. Eithne's book on Irish crochet has been a great help to many learners of Irish crochet throughout the world.

Clockwise:
Old Sprigging on linen muslin collar, with Irish crochet insets
Wooden handled (famine) hook and cotton thread
Satin thread table centre
Dress piece with Shamrock Clones knot filling stitch
Old centre piece – Irish crochet centre with Clones knot and motifs around edge
Courtesy of Daphne D'Arcy from her mother, Eithne D'Arcy's collection
Most of the collection probably came from the McGorry business collection

Our Logo – Eileen McAleer's Three-buttony Shamrock

In 1988, we borrowed our logo from a very nice photo in Eithne D'Arcy's pattern book on Irish Crochet Lace. *We made variations in the pattern, as all lace-makers do, to suit our tension.[71] Eileen McAleer, who worked on the committee of the Lace Guild since 1988, first as treasurer and then helping me to parcel orders, always included the logo among the motifs that she made for the Guild. She taught in the Cassandra Hand Summer School of Clones Lace and also taught her daughters, Grainne and Deirdre, to crochet. They have left it aside for now, while they get on with their busy young lives. I have no doubt that they will return to it, when they have children of their own.*

Make 3 buttonies. Join the buttonies to each other with SSs.

Make 12 CH from an outside point of one buttony to the same point in next buttony and repeat twice
  more, so that you have a circle.

To make leaves of piece, do each one individually, as you would do for petals of flower. Make 18 DCs
  into the first section (from first to second buttony). Turn.

Make 9 loops (4 CH in each loop). Decrease in each row, by turning, and making 2 CH into last loop
  of previous row, then 4 CH loops, SS into next loop of previous row.

Continue until 1 loop remains.

SS and CH 2 down to base and start on second leaf, as for first one. Repeat for third leaf.

Bring in PC, and go around each leaf of piece, with PC, making 2 DCs into each loop of leaf, 4 CH up
  each side18 DC, with 3 P in centre and then 18 DCs down other side. SS into base circle. Repeat for
  all leaves.

Pull PC firm as you finish off each leaf.

Finish off.

*Eileen McAleer and daughter,
Grainne*

MARIAM SAVAGE

Mariam Savage was born and grew up in the countryside outside Ballynahinch, county Down. She is self-taught, and always had a love of lace, although her family has no lace-making tradition. Her Auntie Kathleen was interested in handwork and did drawn thread-work. Mariam can remember an old woman near where she lived sitting outside her cottage doing sprigging (fine white embroidery), just as the women in the Clones area crocheted outside their homes. Mariam now lives in Portadown, county Armagh and does intricate flowers that are very time-consuming. Her work displays a painstaking attention to detail. She takes great pride in her work.

She has spent her lifetime gathering old patterns from second-hand shops. Her search for patterns and ways to improve her techniques has taken her all over Ireland and includes an historic meeting with the late Miss Gunns of Fivemiletown, county Tyrone. She first introduced herself to me some years ago enquiring about threads. After seeing her work, I was very keen to have her work for the lace guild. She has been crocheting for us ever since, though in limited quantities.

While her main interest is in crochet lace she has in the recent past completed other intricate crochet work and some of these have been sent to America, Canada and Australia.

The following flower, which she calls Auntie's Flower, named after her Auntie Kathleen, is one of her more simple motifs. I have transcribed it exactly as she gave it to me.

AUNTIE'S FLOWER

Wrap PC 8 times around a No. 7 knitting needle, slip off, and work
    30 DC into the ring.

First row. * 6 CH, miss 4 DC on ring. 1 DC into next DC. Repeat from
    * 5 times.

Second row. 1 DC, 9 TR, 1 DC into each 6 CH loop.

Third row. 7 CH and 1 DC over each DC of first row, working from
    back to front.

Fourth row. 1 DC, 4 CH, 1 DC, 4 times into 7 CH loop. Turn.

4 CH and 1 DC into each loop, Turn.

4 CH and 1 DC into each loop (3 loops).

Turn. 4 CH and 1 DC into each of 2 loops.

SS loosely down to first DC (under 7 CH).

Take up the packing cord (PC) and work DC closely over it, all
    round the petal.

Drop the packing cord and repeat round the flower.

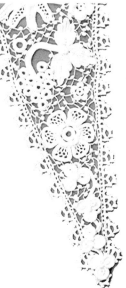

*Hands of
Mariam Savage
crocheting*

Part of collar by Mariam Savage

MARY FARMER'S ROSE LEAF

Mary is an excellent crocheter. She makes all-lace Christening bonnets for us, being among the few people that can fill a piece, using the Clones knot. She is better known in this area, however, as a dressmaker and makes up linen Christening robes and Communion dresses into which we put Clones lace insets. She has also made beautiful wedding dresses to adorn blouse tops. It is a great advantage to work with a dressmaker who is familiar with lace. In 1995, she made hundreds of rose leaves for blouses commissioned by the Irish designer, Lainey Keogh.

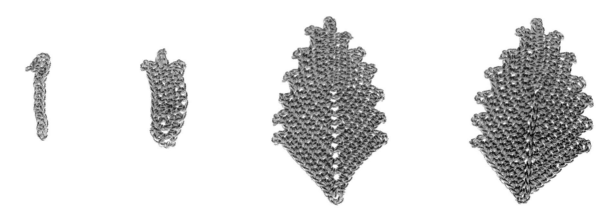

Using the same thread as you have used to make your other motifs, make 13 CH. Turn.

Miss 1 stitch. Make 1 DC in each of 12 stitches.

Make 3 CH alone. Make 1 DC into each DC up other side to last 3 stitches of row. Turn.

3 CH alone. 1 DC into each DC to end of row.

3 CH alone and then 1 DC into each DC up other side of leaf, to last 3 ST.

3CH alone, and turn. 1 DC into each DC of previous row to end.

3 CH (there should be a pattern of holes forming in the centre of the leaves).

Continue in pattern until there are 6 ribs on each side of centre.

Finish at bottom centre of leaf, and pull SS up through each of centre holes of leaf.

Finish off.

These rose leaves are normally used to adorn wild roses.

SMALL LEAF (2)

I worked out this leaf, based on the rose leaf, to go with the clematis or 'other' flowers.

Steps 1–7 are similar to the rose leaf. Steps 8 and 9 take the thorn edge off the leaf, finished with a
    row of packing cord.

16 CH. Turn.

16 DC into CH of previous row. 3 CH alone.

Working up other side of work, crochet 14 DC into backs of DCs of previous row.

Make 1 CH on turn, before crocheting DCs into backs of DCs just made.

3 CH in centre, then repeat stage 5.

Continue, as you did for rose leaf, but with 1 CH on turn of leaf, until you have
    made 6 ribs.

Bring in a small doubled piece of PC and work DCs around leaf with PC, making
    3 DC into top centre of leaf.

Continue to end and finish off.

DAISY

I got the daisy from a wedding dress that I was repairing. I don't know where the dress was originally made, but Elizabeth Monahan was able to show Annetta Hughes how to do the same daisy with the cotton wool centre, so they must have been popular in this area too.

Make 15 DC around PC.

SS last ST to first ST, pulling PC into circle.

Drop PC. Make 5 loops (5CH, SS) around circle. These loops form the bases for the petals.

On first loop, make 6 DC. Turn.

Make 3 loops (4CH. SS). Turn.

Increase to 5 loops on the second row.

Continue for 4 more rows. SS and CH down to base – this completes the first petal.

Continue for 4 more petals.

Using the same PC as for circle, make DCs over PC around the 5 petals – 2 DCs in each loop and SS into circle at the bases of each petal.

Finish off.

CENTRE BUTTON:

You will have to use your own knowledge and imagination to make the button, but perhaps you will find this a guide.

6 CH, SS last ST to first ST.

4 loops (4 CH, SS) into circle.

Make another row of loops.

On third row, increase to 7 loops, by making 2 loops into 1 loop 3 times.

Continue for 4 or 5 rows.

Roll up very small ball of cotton wool and place it in the centre of your work.

Start decreasing, by making 1 row of 3CH loops, then 1 row of 2CH loop – 1CH loops.

When cotton wool is completely covered, attach it to the daisy, with CHs and SSs.

Finish off.

THE THISTLE

The thistle is found commonly in hedgerows around this area. There are several ways of doing the thistle. This is my favourite one and it is quite simple to make.

HEADS OF THISTLE: work around PC for heads.

20 DC around PC. Catch with SS to tenth DC from end, making a circle. Pull PC and turn.

Make DCs into back of these DCs, increasing on circle to keep it flat, working to last stitch. Turn with CH.

* Make 11 DC into back of DCs from previous head. 4 DC around PC alone. Turn with CH. Work into back of DCs just made.

Repeat from * for third head, pulling cord gently each time.

For fourth head, make 11 DC into back of DCs, from previous head. 6 DC around PC alone. Turn with CH.

On downside, miss every second DC, for first half of head. Then, work into every DC, as you did for the other heads. Drop PC.

BODY:

Make 5 of 4 CH loops along bottom of heads.

Continue for 3 more rows. Then start decreasing until 1 loop remains (5 CH on last loop).

Work down side of work with SSs and CHs to PC at base of heads.

To edge thistle with PC, make 2 DC around PC into each loop up right side with 5 DC into top middle loop. Continue with DCs around PC down left side, to end.

Turn and make second row of DCs with PC, around body, with 3 DCs into top centre DC. Continue down to end and finish off.

Attach 'buttony' to bottom centre of body of thistle, if you are making a thistle and fern spray.

The Fern

I first got the fern, with the thistle, from an antique dress that I was asked to repair. There are several types of fern in Irish crochet motifs, but I like this one. There is a fern very similar to this one in an old Clones lace dress front in the Canal Stores, Clones.

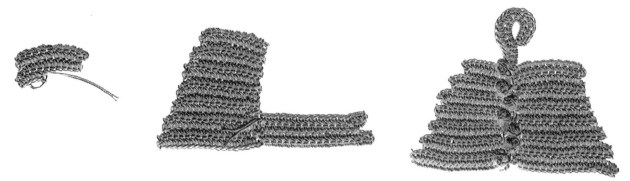

Make one side of the fern first, increasing top to bottom. Then, working from the bottom for second side, work up to top, decreasing. Make top head and finish off with Clones knots down middle of leaves. Work around PC all the time for this fern.

Make 10 DC around PC. Turn with single CH and make DCs into each DC of last row.

* Turn with single CH and make DCs into the back loop of each DC. Do not crochet into the last DC. Increase, by making 2 DCs around PC alone. *

Turn with single CH and continue * to * for 6 more sections, increasing 2 DC in each leaf, until there are approx. 17 DC on seventh leaf.

To make second side of fern:

Crochet 17 DC around PC alone.

Turn with CH and work into the back loop of each DC of previous row, as before.

Then SS in to the seventh row of the first side.

Crochet 15 DC into DCs of previous row. Crochet 1 DC on PC alone (16 DC). Make single CH to turn.

Crochet 16 DC into the back loops of DCs of previous row. SS to fifth row of the first side.

Continue for second side upwards, decreasing each row, rather than increasing. When you get back to middle point, make SS into corresponding leaf on opposite side. (Examine illustrations to understand!)

When you come to top of fern, make 15 DC around PC alone, out of centre of top right and left leaves.

Make circle by crocheting SS to eighth DC from end and pull PC into circle. Turn. Make DCs into back of these DCs, increasing into back of every third DC on circle, as you did for head of thistle. Join with SS to leaves. Drop and cut PC.

Make 5 CKs down middle of leaves. SS each CK into fern as you go along to bottom of fern.

To make fern and thistle spray:

If you want to make spray of fern and thistles, SS into fern and rejoin PC. Crochet 10 DC around PC.

Crochet 2 CH alone and crochet a further 10 DC.

Connect a thistle and turn with CH.

Crochet 10 DC into DCs you have just made.

When you come to 2 CH, make a further 10 DC on PC alone.

Join to second thistle and turn with single CH.

Crochet into DCs you have just made.

When you come to 2 CH, continue with DCs over PC back to fern.

Finish off and cut PC.

Top left: Blouse made by Cassie O'Neill, Aghadrumsee worn by Patricia Crudden.

Top right: Cassie's original blouse was altered by the Cruddens for the wedding top. The skirt was made from an antique bishop's alb by Katie, Annie and Ellen Crudden in the 1980s. This wedding dress is on exhibition in the Ulster Canal Stores, Clones.

Bottom: Dress worn by Damhnait Treanor, 2000. Lace blouse by Máire Treanor, Tessie McMahon and Tessie Leonard.

Top: This wedding dress was especially designed by Bridín Twist, Ennis, county Clare for the Irish Garden at Expo 1990. I made the insets at the front and sleeves. Annetta Hughes made small vine leaves. Eileen McAleer made 200 small roses which Bridín hand-sewed with pearls all over the dress. Elizabeth Monahan made 40 yards of 3-looped edging for the dress. The Irish Garden won first prize in its section. I had been making Clones lace for six months when I worked on this dress.

Below: I made the top of this wedding dress in 1994 for Margaret Comiskey, Dublin.

Top left: Charlene Browne, 1998. Lace top made by Máire Treanor.

Top right: Wedding dress made by Annie, Ellen and Katie Crudden in the 1970s.

Bottom: Niamh Mullally, Rosses Point, Sligo. This dress was bought by Mairead McCartney, an aunt, in New York in the 1940s. I copied some of the motifs when I was asked to repair it.

SOME EDGINGS

THREE-LOOPED EDGING

Before you do these edgings, do the straight row and pillar row on page 91.
See abbreviations on page 51.

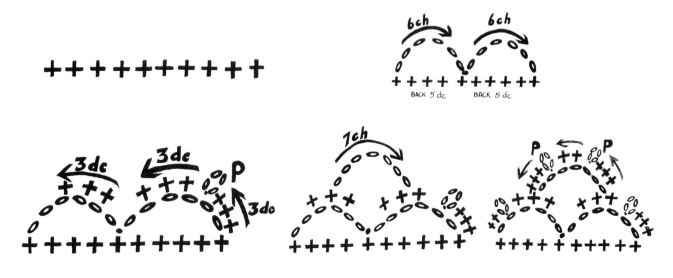

TEN-LOOPED EDGING

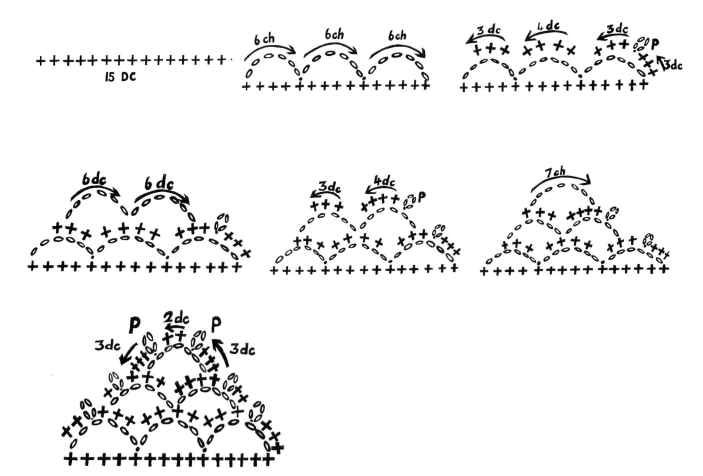

SHAMROCK EDGING

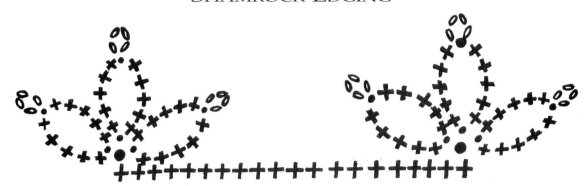

I saw this edging on an old piece in the Sheelin Museum of Lace in Bellinaleck, county Fermanagh.

Do straight row and pillar row on piece first.

Do 20 DCs around 4 strands of PC on next row.

Then separating 2 strands of PC, make shamrock.

Do 2 DC, half TR, 5 TR, P, 5 TR, half TR, 2 DC, SS into first stitch and pull PC.

Repeat for next 2 leaves, completing shamrock.

Do another 20 DC over 4 strands and repeat shamrock.

Continue like this until you have completed the edging.

THE SCROLL

I use this scroll as an edging between larger flowers. It can be used as a motif though, if you wish.

Working over PC, make 25 DC, CH 2 alone (to make division mark), then 15 DC over PC.

Join the last 15 DC with SS, at the division mark. Pull the PC into in a circle.

Drop PC and turn. CH 2, SS into next DC. CH 4 and SS into every second DC, back around circle and
  to end of row.

Turn and make 4 CH loops, catching into previous row and continue back to PC.

Pick up PC and work 27 DC around PC, working 3DC into each loop.

Make three-looped edging – * Crochet 6 CH alone, SS to fourth DC back. Crochet 6 CH, SS to next
  fourth DC back.

Turn. 2 DC into first loop. 4 CH Picot. 3 DC over remainder of loop.

3 DC into next loop. 6 CH alone. SS into DC before picot in next loop.

Turn. 2 DC, P, 2 DC, P, 2 DC.

1 DC into next loop. P, 2 DC. *

DC around PC on main scroll. Work * to * twice more.

Work 2 DCs around PC into each loop, to end of row.

Finish off and cut PC.

HOW TO MAKE, FILL IN AND FINISH OFF A PATTERN

You can make your own collar patterns, using the inside neckline of a blouse, drawing the collar free hand in the shape desired. Likewise, by drawing around plates, round tins, or anything in the required size found in the kitchen, you can make the pattern for centres. I have seen Irish crochet described as 'freeform', because of the way you fill it in a network, without any real pattern to follow, but rather by your own intuition.[72]

Cut out a template, either in curtain lining or brown paper, to the shape that you want.

Select the motifs that you are going to use in the design and crochet one row of Clones knot filling stitch around them.[73] This makes the work a lot easier.[74]

Place the motifs, on the pattern in your own design.

Fill between the motifs with your desired filling stitch. There should be just enough space between the motifs, to join together with 5 CH, SS to CK, then back to another motif. Continue in a criss-cross fashion.

Work out to the edge of the pattern.

Be careful to work right to the edge, going right around the edge of the work and testing it by pulling the knot out with your hook, ensuring that it goes to the edge. Any part that doesn't go out to the edge should be filled. Likewise, make sure not to go over the edge. Use the pattern edge as your guideline.

Crochet a 'straight row' around the pattern depending on the space between the filling. Experience will help you to determine how to do this part.

Crochet a 'pillar row' on the next row around the pattern. Sometimes there will be two DC in each loop. The tension is important in the straight row and at the 'pillar row' stage. Make sure that your piece is lying flat and is nicely rounded off.

For guidelines on 'straight row' and 'pillar row', see page 91.

Make desired edging now.

*1920s style dress with fringes, modelled by
Jacqui Moore MacDonald 1993.*
Dress courtesy of Imelda Kelleher, Dublin

88

WORKING WITH LINEN

TESSIE LEONARD

Tessie has been our most productive worker, since we started our Guild in 1988. I first got to know her in 1988. Having her family reared, she lives in Newtownbutler, county Fermanagh. She works by the light of the window most of the day, covering her day clothes with her apron, crocheting whatever she can do. She edges hankies for other businesses in Portadown and Belfast. She is always available for more work and can 'try her hand at anything'. She says that in the old days, only the best crochet worker in the area used the 'rolled dot' to join and finish off a piece. She learned to do it a few years ago and, although in her late seventies, she is still learning new stitches and new patterns. She uses one of the old wooden-handled hooks made by John Joe McElroy many years ago. She has all the old terms, but admits that she can't read a pattern. Tessie recently tried out one of Pat Mc-Mahon's hooks that I presented to an American CGOA tour group and she asked me to try and get her one, as it had a 'powerful lift to it'.[75]

Her mother, Ellen Connolly, nee McAloon crocheted. Ellen made water lilies at half a crown a dozen in the 1930s. As a child Tessie would have helped her with the 'hearts', roses or shamrocks and the 'clocks' or embellishments for the centre of the lilies. Ellen also did the work that Tessie now does – the rose and shamrock centres, edging linen hankies and inserting insets in linen tableware. Mrs Cunningham used to come to the family home on a Friday to collect the crochet. There 'were a sight of crocheters in the area', according to Tessie. The boys in the family did the 'hearts' when they were children. Her daughter, Louise, has continued her mother's tradition and is also a great crochet worker. In Tessie's younger days, they lived in Aghadrumsee, near where the Cruddens lived. They used to go on 'their céilí' to other houses where the women crocheted around the fire while the men played a game of cards. Ann Kelly nee Crudden remembers Tessie and her sister-in-law, 'Baby', coming on 'their céilí' to their house on a pony and trap! Tessie says that she remembers her grandmother 'peggin', which is a local name for wool crochet, with a bone hook. I have also heard other crochet workers in the area use this term.

A couple of years ago I was making an all-lace top and spent all Sunday joining one sleeve to the body, only realising at the end of the day that I had joined it inside out! I was raging and told Tessie about it the next day. She sat back and declared, with a glint in her eye, 'Crochet on Sunday and poke it out with your nose on Monday!'

Table setting of Irish crochet and linen table mats and napkins, commissioned order for the Bahamas in 1999, crocheted by Tessie Leonard

'Saldin'

'Saldin' (soliding) is the local term used for hand-rolling a straight edge of linen, and crocheting double crochets around the hand-rolled linen. Both Tessie Leonard and the Cruddens crochet the edgings of linen. It is another dying craft as it can be done much quicker, though not as effectively, on a machine. We have always left the linen work to these families, as it is a craft in itself which younger crochet workers like myself have not perfected. Although our crochet workers now get 'punched' hankies from a linen factory in county Armagh, they used to have to poke holes in them, either using a threadless sewing machine or a darning needle. This was the job of the younger members of the family, making it easier to 'sald' the linen with the hook and thread. This method is still used for tray cloths and table cloths.

To cut a piece of linen:

You can simply rip a piece of linen in a straight line. Just snip the piece with scissors where you want it cut. Then rip. It will rip straight because of the weave of the linen.

If you want to cut a small piece for a tray cloth, etc:

Using a pin, loosen a thick thread in the linen, and gently pull right through. If you don't succeed in pulling it all the way through, try again, continuing the thick thread. You can then cut along this line. Alternatively, cut about half an inch of the linen. Rip along this line. About half an inch in from end, pull a second thread, using the pin again. This will be your guideline, as you roll into this line.

Lick thumb and index finger with tongue.

Tightly roll in edge of linen twice, into the line formed by the withdrawn thread, so that no thread is visible.

As you roll, work DCs closely together, put hook through the line from which you pulled the thread. Make approximately 16 stitches per inch.

At the corners, turn the fabric and roll a new edge down next side, overlapping the corner. Make 4 DC into the corner.

Continue around the four edges of the linen piece.

You are now ready to begin the next stage.

Follow instructions for 'Saldin' and pillar row on linen side.
Prepare lace side of work as follows:

To make straight row:

Make 5 CH, TR, 3-4 CH from one loop to next loop.

If you are working around a Clones knot piece, make TR and 2 CH on either side of knot.

Continue around, ensuring that tension is tight, but not too tight, and lies flat.

To work corner, make TR, 8-9 CH, TR on second side. Continue …

When you have completed the straight row, continue second round as directions for pillar row below.

Pillar Row:

This time, your work should be more regular.

Make 5CH, * TR into loop of previous row, 3 CH *. Continue * to * to end.

You are now ready to start edging of your choice.

Clones lace presentation to President Mary McAleese by her Aunt, Kathleen O'Grady of Clones – 1999. Embroidery by Dolores McGuigan, lace by Tessie Leonard and Máire Treanor

Education Ministers – Michael Woods and Martin McGuinness at Gaelscoil Eois – 2001

These are just a few of the pieces of Clones lace that have been presented to visiting state dignitaries over the years. Among those who aren't photographed here are US Presidents, American Ambassadors to Ireland and Australian state officials. Visitors to Clones from as far apart as Japan, various parts of Europe and Alaska, buy Clones lace to bring home. Clones lace is often bought by local people travelling to visit relatives abroad. Especially framed presentation pieces also make exquisite corporate or wedding gifts.

IRISH CROCHET

THE CRUDDENS

The Cruddens are a traditional lace-making family. Three sisters, Ellen, Katie and Annie were great crochet workers living near Magheraveely, county Fermanagh, 'working all the hours that God gave them.' Katie was often seen crocheting in the front passenger seat of the car on her way to Mass on a Sunday morning.[76] The Cruddens are renowned as crochet workers in this area, and are well known for the perfection of their work. Their mother, Brigid McElroy, from the Knocks, was also a well-known crochet worker and one of her collars has become a precious family heirloom. The Cruddens did a lot of work for Mamo MacDonald on her antique Clones lace Church vestments. When the older members of the family died, their daughters carried on the craft.

As children, Brigid, Eileen and Anne made chain necklaces for their holy medals. Brigid was the only one of the sisters to crochet as a young girl. I never knew her, as she died in the 1980s, before I came to Clones. According to Eileen, 'she was a great crocheter and would take on anything, just by looking at it'. Anne and Eileen have been expertly making up our hankies and beautiful fine rose and shamrock centres since the lace guild was formed in 1988. Their sister, Alice joined them in 1995.[77] Ellen Todd, a cousin who has been crocheting for years, also helps them when they get large orders and takes workshops in Irish crochet squares and wool crochet in the Knocks and Lisnaskea. Teresa Reilly, another cousin, used to join the 'pieces' to make table centres, but Alice now does this part, since Teresa's death in 1997.

Eileen's daughter, Irene is now proudly carrying on the family tradition. As well as crocheting for the guild, she 'does up the crochet' that her mother and aunts make. Anne's daughter, Pauline is also

interested in the crochet. Eileen's granddaughter Clara, my daughters, Máiréad and Áine, with their young friend, Tara, also come along and all four are learning the basic crochet stitches. So the tradition is being carried on!

The Cruddens: l–r: Alice, Irene, Eileen and Anne

Eileen and Máire teaching children

Irish Crochet Squares

We call the rose and shamrock squares joined together Irish crochet. Locally, the mitred filling stitch is used to join them – in centres and collars – sometimes this fine work offsets the more elaborate guipure work in blouses. As I have written in other parts of this book, in the folk memory of local people this fine work is Clones lace, as it is what they remember being done at home when they were children. Although these fine squares were made all over Ireland, I don't know of any other area in Ireland where this trellis work, using such fine thread, is made for sale today.

ROSE CENTRE:

6 petals, 2 or 3 rows, depending on preference.

Work as for *Small Rose* on page 60. Do not cut thread, when you have finished rose.

TO MAKE ROSE SQUARE:

SS to top right side of petal.

5 CH. SS back into third CH (picot) 5 CH again. (picot) 2 CH. Catch with SS into left corner of petal.

Repeat this double picot loop (DPL), catching it with SS to right side of next petal. Continue with DPL.s until you have 12 loops around rose.

Squares courtesy of Ann Kelly

4 CH and SS to middle of first loop made. Make 2 DPL.s, catching with SS between Ps of previous row.

To make bar – 6 CH. Catch between Ps of next loop. Turn work. 6 CH, catching with SS back to last loop. Turn work. Make (1 DC, 8 TR, 1DC, SS) into loop just made.

Make 2 more DPLs. Make bar as previous step. *

Repeat * to * until 4 bars are made evenly around rose. Finish row.

If you want to make a 6 row square, continue. Otherwise finish off with your 4 rows.

Repeat as for second row, spacing bars in line with bars of second row.

As for third row of square. Finish off.

TO MAKE SHAMROCK SQUARE:

Follow pattern for 'Shamrock' on page 64, and then make square around shamrock, dividing 3 P loops evenly on each leaf and 1 loop between leaves, to make 12 picot loops.

TO JOIN SQUARES:

Put shamrock and rose motifs face to face.

Join in thread at end of one side of square.

Make 6 CH, P, 2CH and join loop to second square.

Repeat, joining to loop on first square. Join each side alternately (in criss-cross manner) to end of row.

Join each square in this way.

These squares can also be joined in a 'mitred' way.

Mitred Filling

This is a traditional filling stitch, local to this area. For further examples of the mitred filling stitch, see the projects at the back of the book.

Join corners of a rose square and a
 shamrock square with SS.
Work up to next loop, with 3 CH.
4 CH, SS into loop on opposite
 side.
3 CH up to next loop.
4 CH, SS into loop of previous row.
 4 CH, SS into next loop.
3 CH up to next loop.

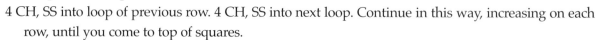

4 CH, SS into loop of previous row. 4 CH, SS into next loop. Continue in this way, increasing on each
 row, until you come to top of squares.
Finish off thread, and join next square, the opposite to what you have beside it, so that you have rose,
 shamrock, rose, etc.
When you have finished this stage and joined all the squares,
Finish off. You should have about 11 loops in mitred part of work.

Laundering Your New Clones Lace

When you have finished your piece of lace, it will probably be quite dirty. Don't worry about this. It is because you have been handling it for so long. If you are experienced in handwork, you probably won't have this problem! Whether it is clean or dirty, it needs to be washed to tighten up the stitches. Always be very careful when laundering a piece of lace and linen, or lace alone. Don't launder a piece of old lace, unless you have discussed it with a museum official.

Put it in an old saucepan and leave it soaking it in your household washing powder overnight.
Soak it in clear water afterwards, especially if the washing powder leaves a blue colour from in the
 piece of lace. This is important, as there may be bleach in the washing powder.
Squeeze it out with your hands, or if it is a large piece, put it in a white pillow case and spin it in the
 washing machine. I put Christening gowns and lace blouses in the delicate wash of the washing
 machine.
When you are finished, pull out each segment with your fingers. You might have to scrub some small
 part if you can't get a stain out, or put soap on it and rewash it.
Use special soap to clean stubborn stains. You will gain confidence at washing it with experience.
To dry it, either hang it out in the sun, place it over a white cloth on a radiator, or hang it in a hot press,
 etc.

To press it:
Place your piece of lace, with the layers of flowers, or embellishments, facing into the ironing board,
 over a white thick towel.
Press it gently and carefully.[78] Pull each petal of the flowers into shape, giving it a three-dimensional
 effect.

Laundering Linen:

Wash it as before.

Take it out, after you have boiled or soaked it.

Put it in the spin wash of the machine, or squeeze the excess water out of it.

When it is dry, press it gently, as for lace.

Some people use spray-starch on linen, but the experienced workers use the traditional powder starch!

Although all lace was traditionally starched in this area, in recent years the Cruddens, our local experts at 'doing-up' linen and lace, have stopped using powder starch as, over a long period it cuts and rots the fabric. Elizabeth Monahan always warns us not to starch a piece that is going to be put away. Pieces look just as nice if they are not starched.

Antique Lace

Antique Clones Lace / Irish Crochet should be treated differently to modern lace. I am not an expert on how to handle old lace, so you are better to get advice from somebody, such as a museum official.

Above: Joan Kelleher in 1931 in a dress made by her aunt

*Below: Celebration 2000. Designed and
made by Máire Treanor*

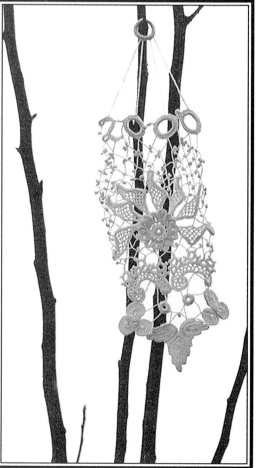

TWELVE PROJECTS

WILD ROSE BROOCH

Designed by Máire Treanor

You will need: one wild rose, one round brooch back.

Make a wild rose. (You can crochet CKs around it, later on,
    if you wish).
With the back of the flower facing, place a brooch back
    with pin on it, in the centre.
Make SS into edge of heart (where centre flower ends).
Make 5 CH across to opposite side.
Make SS to next edge of centre rose.
Make another 5 CH. SS into third side of heart (centre).
Place a brooch back into the centre.
Make 5 CH a third time and SS back at first SS.
Crochet 1 CH alone and cut off thread. Pull the end thread
    tight and fasten off.
Alternatively, you can use clear glue, and stick the brooch back onto the centre of the wild rose.

ROSE COASTER

Designed by Máire Treanor

Crochet: Wild rose, 6 small roses

METHOD:
Make 1 row of filling stitch around each of the flowers.
Draw a circle 4" in diameter on brown paper, or curtain lining and cut out.
Fold circular template in half, then half again.
Run your finger and thumb along these lines, to ensure that they are indented.
Then unfold the circle. These lines help you get the centre lines and quarter lines of the circle.
Place and pin the wild rose in the centre of the circle.
Place and pin the small roses around the wild rose, about 1" apart.
Take off each rose and crochet 1 row of CKs around it.
Tack the roses to the template.
Join the flowers to each other with Clones knot filling stitch, or
    picot filling stitch.
Continue the filling stitch to the edge of the pattern.
When you are ready, make straight row around the pattern.
Continue with Pillar row.
When you have finished the pillar row, start the three-looped
    edging.
When you have completed the coaster, turn it to the back and
    cut off the tacking stitches.
Launder your piece.

WILD ROSE GARDEN
Designed by Máire Treanor

I was inspired to design this piece in 1991 by the Bishop's vestment, which at that time was in Mamo's Lace Gallery. It is now in the Canal Stores. Since making the first one of these, it has become my most popular piece. I now make as many as I can – approximately one or two every month![79] It is the best selling piece in the Canal Stores. Mamo told me a few years ago that when she had occasion to visit Jean Kennedy Smith, who was then the American Ambassador, she noticed one of my framed Wild Rose Gardens hanging in her office. It is popular as a presentation piece. It looks equally well framed, or as a table centre.

Crochet: 7 Wild roses, 6 rose leaves, and 6 scrolls

METHOD:
Prepare a 7" circular template, as in project 2.
Fold the circle in 4 and press with fingers. Place wild rose motif in centre.
Lay out scrolls, wild roses and leaves as shown – pin and tack.
Fill every second section with Clones knots and then the remaining 3 sections. (There are six sections.)
Don't pull the scroll. Your tension will come with experience.
Take the completed piece off the template and launder it.

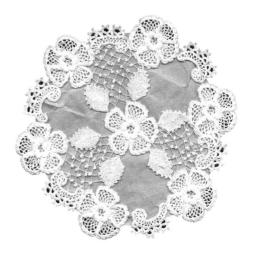

Unfinished wild rose garden

SMALL IRISH ROSE GARDEN
Designed by Máire Treanor

Vera Smyth, who markets Clones lace in the Canal Stores, recently inspired me to design this piece.

Crochet: 6 small roses, 5 scrolls, and 5 small rose leaves, with 4 ribs, rather than 6.

METHOD:

Cut out a 5" centre in curtain fabric or brown paper.

Fold the template centre in 4 and press with fingers. Place a rose in the centre.

Place the 5 roses and scrolls around the outside of the centre and place the leaves below the roses, as shown in illustration.

Tack the motifs down.

Crochet the Clones knot filling stitch between the leaves.

When you have finished, turn over to the back of the template and cut the tacking stitches.

ROSE AND SHAMROCK BASKET
Designed by Máire Treanor

I designed this piece, inspired by a piece in the Canal Stores. Liza Gunn made the centre with the basket of daisies. Annie Crudden, some years later, crocheted a beautiful fine trellis centre piece around it. Although I love the fine trellis work, I prefer to make the corded work. I began by doing daisies in the basket, and making it a piece on its own with Clones knots rather than the original picot filling. A customer then asked me to do shamrocks in the basket. I eventually added roses. Tessie Leonard now crochets this piece for orders. She has added her own individual touch to it. I have also included a photo of one of my 'Basket of Daisies' which I did as a wedding present in 1990.

Crochet: 5 shamrocks, 5 roses, and basket
(The amount of roses and shamrocks depends on the size of your work, and on personal preference. You can also put either roses or shamrocks in the basket.)

METHOD:

Draw around a saucer on brown paper or curtain lining, and cut it out. Fold the circle in 4 and press with your fingers.

Centre the basket and tack it on the pattern with the shamrocks and roses.

Fill in with Clones knots between the basket and on the outside of the basket, to edge of centre.

Do a straight row around circle, ensuring that it keeps the correct tension.

Then make pillar row (3 CH, 1 DC) on second round.

Do three-looped edging. Finish off.

THE BASKET[80]

Make 20 CH. Turn.

Miss 2 CH, DC into each CH of previous row to end. Turn.

2 CH and DC into each DC of previous row to end. Turn.

CH 2, 1 TR into each of next 2 DC. (2 CH, miss 2 DC from previous row.)

* (3 TR, 2 CH) repeat to last 3 stitches. 2 CH and 1 TR. Turn.

2 CH. 2 TR into space of previous row. 2 CH, 3 TR into space. 2 CH. 3 TR into next space. Continue to end of row. 2 CH and 1 TR. Turn. *

Repeat * to * 8 times, creating a basket effect.

For row 13, turn. Repeat as for fourth row to last stitch. 2 CH, 3 TR into last TR. 2 CH. Turn.

2 CH. 2 TR into first TR of previous row. Continue as for previous rows to last stitches.

Make 3 TR into last TR of previous row.

Repeat last row 4 times more, increasing TRs on beginning and end of last row. (17 rows.)

Bring in PC. Make DCs over PC right around outer edge of basket.

Make 3 DCs into each corner.

FOR HANDLE:

On PC alone, make 100 DC. Attach handle with SS to opposite edge of basket. (Make sure that the handle is straight.)

Either keeping the hook in the handle, or if you find it easier, making a large loose SS, stretch DCs out well with your fingers.

Turn and make second row of DCs back over handle, working 2 DCs into every tenth DC.

When you come to end of the handle again, make a second row of DCs over PC around basket, making 3 DCs into each corner DC. Finish off.

THE VINE GARDEN

Designed by Máire Treanor

This piece is very special to me, as I worked on it two months after having suffering serious head injuries in a car accident in 1992. I didn't remember how to play my beloved concertina for a long time afterwards, but Mamo put a crochet hook in my hand in hospital, when I was still very ill and maybe that reminded me subconsciously about lace. This design had been part of my imagination for months before the accident, with the shamrock Clones knot in it. It was the first time I had put the shamrock Clones knot into a piece.

Crochet: 1 Vine leaf, 6 grapes, 6 small vine leaves, 6 scrolls.

METHOD:

Cut out 7″ circular centre.

Fold template in a quarter and press down folds with your finger.

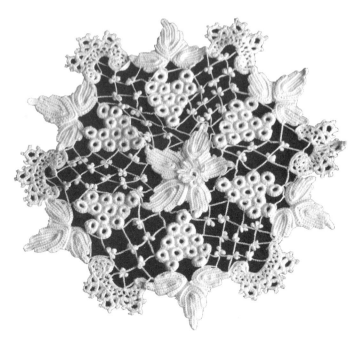

Place vine leaf in centre, with small vine leaves placed evenly around edge, and scrolls between them.

Place grapes below small vine leaves.

Tack all the motifs down.

Work shamrock Clones knots between the motifs. To make Shamrock Clones knot: work CK, 2 CH, CK, 2 CH, CK,2 CH. SS third CK between first and second CK. Work 9 CH between shamrock Clones knots.

When you have finished, take the work off the pattern and launder it.

THE CLEMATIS GARDEN
Designed by Máire Treanor

Daphne D'Arcy kindly lent me some of her mother's old pieces of lace to photograph for this book. On examination of a daisy piece, which I had offered to repair, I noticed that the Clones knot was worked in a different way to any that I had seen before. The worker had made 2 Clones knots into each loop in the same way that double picots would be made rather than single picots. Using this inspiration, I created the following piece.

You will need:
7 clematii and 6 leaves.

Use the same 7″ template centre that you have used for the Wild rose garden.

Fold it in half, then half again, to get centre of pattern.

Place 1 clematis in centre, then 6 around edge of pattern, interspersed with leaves.

With centre clematis in hand, work (4 CH, CK, 4 CH, CK, 4 CH, SS) for 4 or 5 rows.

When CKs touch outside clematii, tack down flowers to template and continue until you fill in centre piece.

CLONES LACE CHRISTENING BONNET

Use 40 cotton thread for motifs and edging and 50 cotton thread for filling stitch. Cotton thread is soft to the baby's head, but if it is not available, use mercerised 40 and 60 or 60 and 80 thread. Use a .50 or .60 hook.

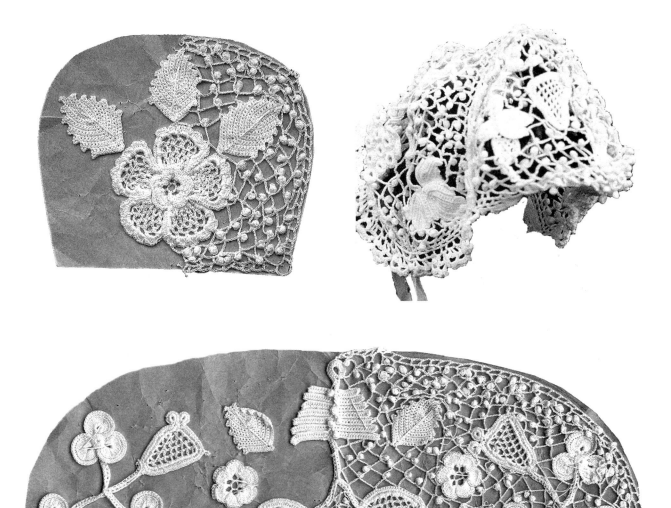

FOR SIDES AND TOP OF HEAD:

2 Shamrock and harp sprays

3 Small roses

3 Rose leaves

1 thistle and fern spray – joined in same way as shamrock and harp spray

FOR BACK OF BONNET:

1 wild rose

3 rose leaves

METHOD:

Make rectangle 9" x 4" for newborn to six-month-old baby. Make it an inch or so bigger for a bigger baby.

Make back piece 3" x 4", as illustration.

Make 1 row of CKs around each motif. The sprays are more difficult to work. Make chains and CKs, where there is space, between sprays. Study illustration. Pin and tack motifs to pattern, as in illustration.

Join CKs to each other, with CHs. Fill in pattern. Each person's tension will be different and it is impossible to direct this freeform type of work. Using your hook, pull the CKs out to the edge.

Do straight row around pattern. TR, 5 CH, TR … all around

Do pillar row around straight row.

Join back of bonnet to straight line of larger piece with SSs and CHs.

Edge around bonnet and around back, using three-looped edging.

CLONES LACE V-NECK COLLAR

Designed by Máire Treanor

Crochet: 2 shamrock sprays, 2 wild roses, 4 grapes, 1 vine leaf, 2 small vine leaves 2 clematii, 2 rose leaves, 2 small roses, 1 shamrock

METHOD:

Place them on the template and work one row of Clones knots around each motif, before tacking them to the template.

Join with CKs and fill in to edge of template.

Crochet straight row.

Crochet pillar row.

Make three looped edging around collar.

Cut tacking off template and wash.

Pull out each segment and dry over cloth.

ROSE AND SHAMROCK MITRED COLLAR
Traditional Design

This is a traditional way of joining collars and centre pieces in the Clones area. Once you are able to do the mitred effect between the squares, you can use the same effect to do a centre piece.

Crochet: 1 rose, 4 row squares, 5 shamrock 4 row squares

METHOD:

For mitred filling follow directions on page 96. Take one rose and one shamrock square and place them on their top side, in diamond shapes. You will need 9 squares to fit an adult, 7 to fit a child. This may vary, according to the size of the neck. You can fit it at this stage.

Crochet Pillar row, continue along all around work to end.

Turn. 5 CH, DC, 2 CH, DC, 2CH … Continue like this to end of row of neckline of collar – second pillar row.

Continue around rest of collar, with 3 CH, 1 DC, 3 CH. Crochet 9 CH on outside corners of squares. DC into mitred corner, keeping its shape.

Tessie McMahon's trellis collar with mitre filling

You should have 2 rows of pillar row around squares and 3 rows on top neck side. For neck side, make 3 DC, 4 CH picot, 3 DC, 4 CH picot … Continue like this to end of row. (Salding.)

Edge round the mitred edged with 3-looped edging, or you can use 3-looped edging all around collar, as illustration.

Finish off.

ROSE AND SHAMROCK TABLE CENTRE
Traditional Design

I don't do this work myself and those who do it don't follow patterns, but work as their mothers taught them. Alice Carey (nee Crudden) helped me to work out this pattern. Examine the photo if you have trouble following this pattern.[81] Those that are adventurous can try out the oval centre piece, from the photograph on page 8 of the colour section. I don't have directions for it, though.

Crochet: 5 shamrock squares, 5 rose squares, 5" circle with rose centre.

Do mitred filling, as you did for the collar above, joining last square to first square. Do not cut thread.

Crochet 10 CH. SS into next loop anti-clockwise.

Crochet 3 DC into CHs just made and crochet 8 CH.

* SS into next loop to right, anti-clockwise.

Crochet 3 DC into CHs, and crochet 8 CH. *

Repeat * to * until you have worked around complete circle, returning to where you started.

Crochet 3 CH to first loop.

Crochet DCs right around CHs on outer circle.

FOR INNER CIRCLE (CENTRE PIECE):

Begin in same way as square, but on second row, make 5 bars rather than 4. Continue as you did for the square, for 10 rows, alternating where you put the bars.

When you have completed circle, so that both inner and outer circles nearly fit together (with about half an inch to spare) do 2 rows of the pillar row on outer circle.

On outside row, make 2 CH, TR, into each loop … 8 CH, TR on corners all round outer edge of squares.

Join centre to outer part with chains and slipstitches.

Edge with 3-looped edging.

Finish off.

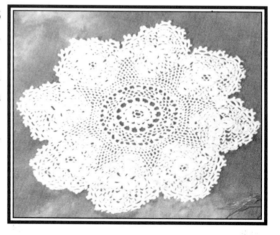

HAND-EDGED HANDKERCHIEF, WITH INSET
Designed by Ellen Crudden

Eileen Crudden says that her mother, Ellen, called this insert the 'm-ee' edging, because it was the shape of an 'm'. Some people also insert small squares into hankies, but I think you'll agree that this type of square, traditionally made by the Cruddens, is more impressive.

Crochet: 4 rounds of a shamrock or rose square, with plain chain loops rather than picot loops

3 CH SS to loop. See scan. Repeat twice more. Turn. Repeat this row 4 times. Finish off.

Join thread on opposite side (see scan) and repeat step 2.

Crochet 5 CH, TR into loop. * 3 CH,TR* Repeat * to* around inset. On each corner, crochet 8 CH, TR.

On second round, crochet 3 CH, TR, 3 CH TR. Continue, keeping tension straight, by crocheting 2 TR into loop of previous row, when necessary.

To attach to hankie, follow directions on page 91. Tack square to hankie. Then cut away half an inch from tacking around squares. Roll in edging, and top sew.

FOOTNOTES

1 I feel that Cork crochet lace deserves an in-depth study and pattern book, such as I am doing here for Clones lace.

2 Boyle, Elizabeth, *Irish Flowerers*, Ulster Folk Museum, 1971.

3 The whitewash brush started life as a thistle.

4 Thelma Goldring was awarded the Churchill Fellowship in 1983, winning a visit to Burano Island, Venice, to study the similarities between Venetian point lace and Clones lace. She spoke at the Sarah Martin Lecture, as part of the *Cassandra Hand Summer School* in 1993 on her very interesting study.

5 This habit still persists. When visitors enter, the lace is put away. I know of a woman who crocheted blouses in her latter days and her daughter never knew it!

6 I got most of my patterns by copying old motifs in garments that I was asked to repair.

7 These are local terms. The 'fine work' refers to the rose and shamrock squares, whereas the 'heavy' or 'coarse work' refers to the floral corded work.

8 I have also recently seen examples of this fine trellis work with the mitred filling stitch, which is common to the Clones area, in two areas where young women were sent by the Congested Districts Board to the west of Ireland around the turn of the twentieth century – in Bruckless, county Donegal and in Cliffoney, county Sligo.

9 The Clones lace class made the original dress for my first daughter Máiréad in 1989, before I started making Clones lace myself. I used the edging for Áine's dress in 1990.

10 MacDonald, B., *A Time of Desolation*, Clogher Historical Society, Monaghan, 2001, p. 8.

11 In 2002, the population of Clones parish, which includes part of county Fermanagh, is over 2000!

12 This embroidery was locally named 'sprigging' and employed a lot more people at the turn of the century than did crochet, throughout Ireland, according to *Irish Flowerers* by Elizabeth Boyle .

13 Family nicknames such as the 'Sprigger' McMahons, confirm this tradition.

14 This money is still used in prizes at the RDS Craft Fair today.

15 According to Susan McDonnell, her ancestor of the same name, attended classes in the rectory to learn the skill of Clones lace from Mrs Hand.

16 I would say this must be a very conservative estimate. It was possibly closer to 15,000, as at the same time there were 12,000–20,000 people crocheting in Cork. The population in the Clones area was over 22,000 and almost every family crocheted!

17 Boyle, Elizabeth, *Irish Flowerers*, Ulster Folk Museum, 1971, p. 53.

18 This building was later named 'The Boardrooms' and used by the Church of Ireland Vestry. It is sometimes referred to as the 'Round Tower Schoolhouse' in historical documents.

19 The rectory was later named Bishopscourt, as the Col Bishop D'Arcy lived there for a few decades.

20 Exact date unknown.

21 There is a copy of this letter in the lace exhibition, which was compiled by Mamo MacDonald with the expertise of members of Clones ICA in the Canal Stores, Clones.

22 Not very likely! It is more possible that this referred to French 'replica' lace, so called because it replicated Irish lace and was sold at very low prices.

23 Boyle, Elizabeth, *Irish Flowerers*, Ulster Folk Museum, 1971.

24 Boyle, Elizabeth, *Irish Flowerers*, Ulster Folk Museum, 1971.

25 Boyle, Elizabeth, *Irish Flowerers*, Ulster Folk Museum, 1971.

26 Boyle, Elizabeth, *Irish Flowerers*, Ulster Folk Museum, 1971.

27 Tess Daly kept this shop open as a tourist outlet from 1951 until Christmas 2001.

28 In Clones, we make commissioned wedding tops and blouses in this traditional way. Pieces were joined most often with the picot filling stitch throughout Ireland.

29 *The Sisters' Connection with the Clones Crochet Industry*, Sisters of St Louis Convent, Clones.

30 Máiréad Dunleavy, National Museum of Ireland.

31 'Buttonies' is the local name for crocheted buttons. The 'hearts' were rose or shamrock, which made up the centre of the squares. A 'piece' was a 'motif'.

32 McGinnity, Annie, 'A History of Crochet in the Roslea/Clones/Aghadrumsee Area', *Roslea Historical Journal*, 1994. Also recollections of Rosaleen Quigley, Clones, 2002.

33 My father's cousin Bridget Connolly remarked that 'the one (daughter) that smoked a pipe, crocheted!' Also recollections of her sister, Roseanne Leonard, Newbliss.

34 Murnane, J. & P., *At the Ford of the Birches*, The Murnane Brothers Publications, p. 247.

35 Kathleen Cassidy, Clones speaking about her grandmother.

36 'Crochet' Betty Connolly, speaking about her grandmother, *Roslea Historical Journal*, 1992.

37 *The Sisters' Connection with the Clones Crochet Industry*, Sisters of St Louis Convent, Clones. I don't agree. I would say that the farmers of Roslea realised that lace-making was the bread earner for the family and were prepared to share duties.

38 To go on your 'céilí' comes from the Gaelic term and tradition to go visit and party at a neighbour's house. They usually took turns at going to each other's houses.

39 Murnane, J. & P., *At the Ford of the Birches*, The Murnane Brothers Publications, p. 382.

40 Her daughter Tessie recently retired after crocheting with us for ten years. She is a beautiful neat worker, whose

work needs to be washed only to tighten up the stitches. She did both types of crochet – the various motifs and the fine trellis collars and centre pieces.

41 In 1997 Mary, who has been coming to my workshops since 1991, asked me to make a bonnet for her baby's Christening, using silk thread that had been found in her Aunt Nancy's flat in Dublin after she died. This silk thread came from Rose's collection. Carmel Lynagh, a friend of mine, now owns Rose's house. A few years ago, Carmel came over to me and asked me to send an old piece of lace to Mary. She had found it while doing work to the bathroom in the house. This was the room that Rose used as the washroom.

42 Mamo set up the Clones Lace Gallery in part of her shop, displaying pieces of lace that she had collected over the years. This was a great attraction to visitors from all over the world for several years, until her retirement in 1995. Her lace collection is now the main attraction in the Ulster Canal Stores, Clones.

43 The Rathfriland area of county Down is famous for its drawn threadwork.

44 The letter explained that Mrs McGahern was applying to the Health Board for the blind pension and that she had given Mrs McGorry's name as her employer for embroidery work.

45 Recollections of Olive Byrne, niece of Mary Kilcoyne.

46 According to local lore, Queen Mary wore it on her coronation in 1906–7, but research by Roslea Crochet Guild disputes this claim.

47 Rosina taught Irish crochet to the local branch of the ICA.

48 Brigid was the grandmother of Joe McElvaney, Monaghan County librarian, Clones.

49 Brenan, James, *The Modern Irish Lace Industry*, 1902, p. 428–9.

50 'Point Irlandaise' as Irish crochet was referred to in France, was very popular there throughout the nineteenth century.

51 *The Democrat and Peoples Journal*, 19 February 1910.

52 This 'chemical lace' was similar in appearance to the handcrocheted lace, but lacked the substance and feel of the handmade product. It was assembled by making lace on a machine or loom in a full piece and then burning off the background using acid.

53 *Victoria*, spring 1993.

54 Veronica Stuart explained at our 2001 Summer School that it was easier to turn lace thread ecru with tea, so that it could be washed white again if need be, than make the piece with ecru thread.

55 If you are using mercerised No.20 thread for the motifs, use No. 40 for the filling stitches, and No. 20 for the edging.

56 Pat McMahon died on 3 December 2001.

57 Some of them have been lent to the Ulster Canal Stores for exhibition.

58 I recently saw a blouse made by Mrs Quaile, which she had given to Mary Carron, who visited her as a teenager in the 1960s.

59 An Grianán, the national headquarters of the association, in county Louth, organises residential courses in all the laces of Ireland.

60 This work is now in the Ulster Canal Stores, Clones.

61 The joint Summer School 'Celebrating Lace' commemorated 150 years since the Irish famine, and celebrated the introduction of the two laces in county Monaghan.

62 Unfortunately, Lillie recently left her lampshade in a taxi, while going to a lace class in Dublin. She had been working on it for years, bringing it to classes both in Clones and Dublin.

63 Mary Shields, author of *Lasadóireacht: A Practical Workbook for Carrickmacross Lace*, Wee Hills Publications, 1992.

64 Right-handed people call us 'cittars' from the Gaeilge 'citeogaí'. Don't mind them. We are more artistic!

65 Mary McErlain, in my workshop in Ballymaguigan, said that I reminded her of her brother. He used a thrawl to put cement on bricks. He thrawled along to the end of the row with his left hand. He then put it in his right hand and thrawled back to the end on the next row.

66 Basket of daisies by Liza Gunn. Her niece Elizabeth Monahan gave the Cruddens a box of Liza's old motifs. The Cruddens then crocheted squares around it.

67 Recollections of Olive Byrne, whose aunt, Mary Kilcoyne, was a lace buyer.

68 Recollections of her family, Tommy, Annie and Bridget.

69 Recollections of Olive Byrne.

70 I was recently asked to have a blouse made by her cousin, Judith, who lives in Canada. Eithne got one made for her in the 1960s.

71 Clones lace-making is like other forms of our tradition. We always change a pattern, making it our own.

72 Cosh, Sylvia & Walters, James, *The Crochet Workbook*, St Martins Press, 1989.

73 Cassie Mc Quaid who lives outside Scotstown, was the first person I ever saw doing this.

74 Kathleen Quigley remembers that her mother said she got ideas for her patterns by looking at her wallpaper.

75 CGOA = Crochet Guild of America.

76 When Brian MacDonald read this section, after reading Tessie Leonard's piece, he asked did she poke it out with her nose?!

77 She was inspired by our visit to President Mary Robinson during the 'Celebrating Lace' Summer School in 1995.

78 Some feel that even modern crochet should not be pressed, as this destroys the three dimensional intention of the lace. Personally, I always like to press my lace lightly, face downwards, over a towel.

79 In the past, Tessie McMahon made the wild roses and scrolls. I made the leaves and the Clones knot filling stitch. Since Tessie's retirement, Raeleen Reavy has agreed to make the wild roses. I couldn't make the whole piece in

the time that the Ulster Canal Stores and the customer needs them. This is the way Clones lace was traditionally done.

80 Breda Bohan, who attended the Summer School regularly in the first years, first wrote out the basket pattern. I made it from memory until then.

81 This image does not exactly match the directions given.

SOME IRISH CROCHET PUBLICATIONS

Boyle, Elizabeth, *Irish Flowerers*, Ulster Folk Museum, 1971.

Cartier-Bresson, *Fine Irish Crochet Lace*, Dover Needlework Series, Priscilla Publishing Co., 1994.

D'Arcy, Eithne, *Irish Crochet Lace*, Colin Smythe Publications and Dolmen Press, 1984, 1990.

De Dillmont, Therese, *Masterpieces of Irish Crochet Lace*, Dover Needlework Series, Priscilla Publishing Co., 1986.

Shimura, Fumiko, *Irish Crochet Lace*, Japan, 1997, ISBN4–529–02889–5.

Irish Crochet Techniques and Projects, Dover Needlework Series, Priscilla Publishing Co., ISBN 0–486–24705–8, Republished by Mineola, New York, 1984.

Kliot, Jules & Kaethe, *Irish Crochet Lace Instruction and Design*, Lacis Publications Berkley, California, 1980, 1983. ISBN 0–916896–17–X.

Maidens, Ena, *The Technique of Irish Crochet Lace*, B. T. Batsford Ltd, London, ISBN 0 7134 4491 6.

Mensinga, Nan, *How to do Irish Crochet*, American School of Needlework Publication, 2000, ISBN 0–88195–938–5.

Potter, Annie Louise, *A Living Mystery: The International Art and History of Crochet*, A. J. Publishing International, 1990, ISBN 1–879409–00–3.

USEFUL PUBLICATIONS

MAGAZINES & PAMPHLETS:

McCarthy, Maolíosa, 'Linked by a Thread', Pamphlet of Clogher Historical Society, 1997.

Piecework, July/August 1997.

Victoria, Spring 1993 p. 36–38.

McGinnity, Annie, 'A History of Crochet in the Roslea, Clones, Aghadrumsee area' in *Journal of Roslea Historical Society*, 1994, p. 15–19.

BOOKS:

Irish Homestead, January 1897.

Baines, Patricia, *Spinning Wheels: Spinners and Spinning*, B. T. Batsford, 1977, ISBN 0 7134 0822.

Cathcart, Rosemary, *The Sheelin Antique Irish Collection*, 1999.

Collins, Brenda, *Flax to Fabric: The Story of Irish Linen*, An Irish Linen Centre & Lisburn Museum Publication, 1994.

Connolly, Sybil, *Irish Hands*, Hearst Books, New York, 1994.

Cosh, Sylvia & Walters, James, *The Crochet Workbook*, St Martins Press, 1989.

Klickman, Flora, *The Craft of the Crochet Hook*, circa 1906, out of print.

Longfield, Ada K., MA LLB, *Guide to Collection of Lace*, out of print.

MacDonald, Brian, *A Time of Desolation: Clones Poor Law Union 1845–50*, Clogher Historical Society, 2001.

Moodie, Vicki (ed.) *Learn to Crochet: Left and Right-Handed Instructions Made Easy*, Craft Moods Publication, ISBN 1–876373–05–9.

Shields, Mary, *Lasadóireacht: A Practical Workbook for Carrickmacross Lace*, Wee Hills Publications, 1992.

Stuart, Veronica & Catherine, *Patterns and Guidelines for Irish Laces*, published by V & C Stuart, 1996.

Stuart, Veronica, *The Revival of Youghal Needlepoint Lace*, published by Veronica Stuart, 1992.

SOME WEBSITES

http://www.clones.ie

http://www.irish-lace.com

http://www.crochet.com

http://www.craftscouncil-of-ireland.com

http://www.craftireland.com

http://clogherhistoricalsoc.com

http://www.mercier.ie

NOTES